WRITING ON THE MOON

WRITING ON THE MOON

Stories and Poetry from the Creative Unconscious by Psychoanalysts and Others

Edited by
Bonnie Zindel

Routledge
Taylor & Francis Group

LONDON AND NEW YORK

First published 2017 by Karnac Books Ltd.

Published 2018 by Routledge
2 Park Square, Milton Park, Abingdon, Oxon OX14 4RN
711 Third Avenue, New York, NY 10017, USA

Routledge is an imprint of the Taylor & Francis Group, an informa business

British Library Cataloguing in Publication Data

A C.I.P. for this book is available from the British Library

ISBN-13: 9781782204602 (pbk)

Typeset by V Publishing Solutions Pvt Ltd., Chennai, India

For David and Lizabeth
and
In Memory of Mannie Ghent

CONTENTS

ACKNOWLEDGEMENTS

Many thanks to the editors of *Psychoanalytic Perspectives*, who have supported my vision and given me the space to create something new in a scholarly journal. I also want to express deep appreciation for the extraordinary education and clinical training I received at my professional home, the National Institute for the Psychotherapies in New York—and to all my friends and colleagues in the NIP community.

I'm extremely grateful to Rod Tweedy, my editor at Karnac, for believing in this book and bringing his gifted hands to the project. Thanks also to Kate Pearce, Cecily Blench, Constance Govindin, and James Darley at Karnac, who all made important contributions.

I'm indebted to Amanda Ashworth, publisher of *Psychoanalytic Perspectives* at Routledge, for her creative enthusiasm and for sharing her love of Wordsworth—and to production editor Leah Cutler, who has been a steady and meticulous hand.

To Mannie Ghent, my training analyst, who encouraged my rebirth, and who read to me from treasured books in his library, especially the poems of Jacques Prevert and Ovid's *Metamorphosis*.

I am especially grateful to Thomas Ogden, who embodies the essence of creative vitality. We share a love of literature and writing. He has been a trusted source of inspiration, and I deeply value our friendship.

To Spyros Orfanos, who exudes the spirit of Zorba the Greek, for his innovative creativity study group—and to my fellow creative travelers. To Jody Davies, and the gifted women in our study/supervision group, for their intuition and generosity.

I also wish to thank Julie Grenet, not only a psychoanalyst but also a French scholar, who translated the letters of Proust, Flaubert, and George Sand. And thanks to Allison Katz for her generous assistance.

Special appreciation to my patients and supervisees, who have enriched my life more than they know.

Many thanks also to the members of the creative writing groups I have run over the past twenty years. I am in awe of the risks they take every time they write.

Heartfelt thanks to my dear friends through the years for their love, friendship, and hours of soul-searching and laughter: Nancy Spanier, my creative co-conspirator since we were thirteen years old, Janine de Peyer, Ida Dancyger, Ellen Fries, Caryn Sherman-Meyer, Joyce Selter, Puja Hall, Judith Lit, Pam Frost, Renee Hertzberg, and Constance Cohen.

And to my family. My caring father who always loved me for just being me; he taught me to value my mind and instilled the importance of lifelong intellectual curiosity. And to my mother who encouraged me to dream in many important ways. And to my late big brother, Vic, who is dearly missed.

I feel immense indebtedness to my late husband Paul Zindel for encouraging me to be a writer, and for his brilliant appreciation of drama and language. He was the ultimate artist, and the best person at surprises and the unexpected. He gave freely of his knowledge and talent, and I am eternally grateful.

To my son David, whose adventurous spirit and playful sense of humor have always made me smile and see the world in a new way. To Rachel Zindel, a dynamic and creative force as both actress and mother. And to the littlest Zindels, Dylan Paul and Wyatt Andrew: the future awaits you.

To my daughter Lizabeth, a beautiful, joyous spirit and gifted novelist. Our conversations are a fountain of imaginative ideas, and together we enter a terrain where all becomes possible.

And to Steve Bello, the best of editors. He more than anyone has listened to my ideas, explored them with me, and helped germinate the seeds.

Finally, my heartfelt thanks to all the writers who have submitted poetry, short stories, and nonfiction to the Creative Literary Section over the past fifteen years. And to the contributors whose excellent writing makes up this collection—this book honors your work.

And special thanks to the great unknown!

B.Z.

ABOUT THE EDITOR

Bonnie Zindel, LCSW, a psychoanalyst in private practice in New York, is a faculty member, supervisor, and training analyst at the National Institute for the Psychotherapies. A founding editor and creative literary editor of *Psychoanalytic Perspectives*, she is the author of numerous articles on creativity. She is the author of "A Bird that Thunders: An analysis with Emmanuel Ghent", in *Clinical Implications of the Psychoanalyst's Life Experience* (Routledge, 2013). Bonnie has conducted writing groups for psychotherapists for over twenty years and has conducted writing workshops at international conferences in Rome, Madrid, and San Francisco. *The New York Times* said, "She runs what may be the most nurturing writing group on the literary scene." A playwright and novelist (HarperCollins, Viking, Bodley Head), Bonnie is a former member of the Actors Studio Playwrights Unit. She has most recently written a play, *My Simone*, based on the life of Simone de Beauvoir, which was recently performed in New York.

This book is fifteen years in the making and it is about imagination and originality—two crucial elements in our creative life—and the ability to magically rearrange memories and emotions that have been stored away in some deep and unworded place. Young children have direct access to their creative unconscious and a touch of wonderment. But many of us lose some of that ability as we get older and become more constrained and concrete—and perhaps frightened of that playful part of ourselves.

The creative unconscious, this estuary of the unknown, is the doorway to our originality. It can surface when we least expect it—translating chaos and feelings from our body into poetry, stories, paintings, and music. Here is the Holy Grail, the unworded and mysterious place, the center of our vitality. Here we are old and we are new, existing outside of time. It is our truest nature.

In this place, thunderbolts strike and flying shadows lurk and golden arrows soar. Beware, however, the creative unconscious won't be told what to do. Or be demanded upon. But when it speaks, be ready to translate the untranslatable. Inside this magic cauldron lies the very beast of curiosity, and holds me in its enchantment and nightmares. It is a resplendent bridge to my ancestors, to my mother's grandfather's mother's mother. Wordsworth and Emily Dickinson breathed in these ethers, as did DaVinci. Mozart heard its call.

As this book meanders through unconscious terrain, the questions are: how can we be more originally ourselves? How can we let go of the constraints that bind us? And also get a little messy, embracing mistakes and surprises along the way. Creativity is chancy. Art is chancy. To embrace our creativity is to embrace change. And encourage wonder.

When I was a young girl I would spend hours in my large walk-in closet, playing with my imagination. I would put on my glasses and my wooly cape, and I would make up stories of traveling across the desert to live in a small Bedouin town, selling exotic perfumes. Or turning jewels into meteor showers. I would consult elders about secret watering holes, which led to narrow trails and berry patches. The elders scratched a map in the dirt and showed me where quicksand hid and monsters lurked.

When I returned to my room and put on my wide-awake hat, hours had passed. And in that slip of time, I had entered the timeless place of creativity. I did not know it then but I was in a sacred place—my creative unconscious—where things rattle deep inside; a place of plaster and clay, of warm pools of humanity, all beyond my conscious knowing.

Another important step came in my junior year in high school when Mrs. Lave took me out of Miss Nehren's geometry class, where I couldn't tell the difference between a hypotenuse and a trapezoid, and put me in a new class she was forming on mythology. There I had no trouble remembering all the muses of lyric poetry, dance, imagination, and the celestial sky, the ancient scary creatures, and the twelve gods and goddesses on Mt. Olympus. These days, I like to remember that the gods are far from perfect. If I put Zeus on the couch, I would learn about his unusual traumatic birth, springing from the head of Cronus, his difficult childhood filled with danger, a stormy and jealous union with his wife and sister, Hera—when angry, he would hurl thunderbolts.

After college where I majored in psychology, I started writing plays, screenplays, and novels. I would ask my creative unconscious for help, but it refused to be cajoled or yield to demand. Then when I would least expect it, a new idea would appear in all its glory, and I would stop what I was doing and listen. To make an apple pie from scratch, you must first invent the universe, said Carl Sagan, an astrophysicist. Each time you are creative, you must start from scratch.

After my years as a writer, having published three novels and written three produced plays, I wanted a job that wasn't so lonely and where my just being present was crucial. In the early 1990s, I was with my family in the Caribbean for Easter vacation. I happened to pass a woman on the beach and we began talking. In the five minutes we conversed, she told me about a graduate program she had attended to become a psychotherapist. Upon returning to New York, I applied to graduate school at Columbia University, and my life changed. Eventually I become a psychoanalyst—and I never even learned her name.

During the four-year program at NIP, I felt that I could not serve two masters. So while my literary writing was put on hold, my analyst, Mannie Ghent, and I did share a creative play-space. As part of my training analysis, it was a prerequisite to be in therapy. I would bring in fragments of creative work to Mannie, and he would close his eyes and listen as if he was listening to a dream. Following each session I would go to a café and write scribbled notes on the session. He seemed to open up the buried parts of me. The ritual: always writing. I *am* a writer, and it seems like I have no choice but to write.

In 2001 I was part of a group at my institute planning to start a new scholarly journal. It was important to me to create a permanent space for creative expression. This was an unorthodox idea. It had never been done before. While psychoanalysis had long been interested in creativity, no journal had previously made space for it. I am enormously grateful that the editors were open to taking this leap with me. The Creative Literary Section made its debut in the first issue of *Psychoanalytic Perspectives* in 2003—and has continued to be part of the journal for each of its thirty-one issues to date.

As creative literary editor, I started the first issue with only three poems. The second issue consisted of a poem by Thomas Ogden, whom I had gotten to know through our mutual interest in creative writing. Alongside his poem was a poem by his niece, Emily.

For the third issue I was puzzled. I needed to cast a wide net. I wanted people in the field—and beyond—to know there was now a space for previously unpublished poetry and creative nonfiction in the journal. Our institute had a list-serve, and so did many other institutes across the country. Why not send out a call for submissions that would reach thousands of potential contributors both here and abroad? I put out a call for submissions of "Poetry by people in analysis." The response was overwhelming. Hundreds of poems poured in from as far away as Australia, South Africa, England, France, Scotland, Israel, Canada, New Zealand, and across the United States.

Suddenly, I was faced with a dilemma: how to select the eight or ten poems that I had space to publish. What criteria would I use? I am not a literary scholar. I have no training in critical theory. I am a psychoanalyst and a writer. I have spent the better part of my life studying the craft of writing, and I write creatively almost every day. Thinking about the creative process is a passion, and I have found, at last, that I can serve two masters: psychoanalysis and writing. And I love them both. How did my psychoanalytic sensitivity affect what I responded to? I decided to trust my creative intuition. Did I respond emotionally to the poem? Was I moved? Did it feel original? Did I want to read it again? Did the writers allow me into their being? The feedback on the third issue was very encouraging. Psychotherapists told me how meaningful it was to have this place to bring another part of themselves. And readers told me how much they enjoyed the themes and selections. I realized I was onto something, and in the years ahead, I put out many other calls that stimulated the imagination: "Dreams as poetry," "Love calls—a call for love," "Strong women's voices." In the call for "Mothers of the Milky Way" I said, "Mothers come in complex ways. Surprise us." You will see the fruits of these calls throughout the book. Two-thirds of the contributors are psychoanalysts and psychotherapists. The other twenty-nine contributors are patients, artists, poets, writers, performers, professors, and cartoonists.

The ideas for the calls came from my creative unconscious and leapt into the red-hot embers that animated the creative unconscious of many others. The *Notes from the Creative Literary Editor* that I began to write for each issue are also unconscious collaborations. This is what Shakespeare called "epiphenomenology," where one person's idea sparks another and another—like shooting stars. When these sparks happen, the ideas are combustible. The outpouring of submissions and the quality of the work have been extraordinary. I am thrilled to preserve some of the best of these shooting stars in *Writing on the Moon*.

Bonnie Zindel
www.bonniezindel.com

Pre-Natal Memory, 1941.
Photograph of Salvador Dali by Philippe Halsman.

CHAPTER ONE

Dreams as poetry

You see things, and you say, "Why?" But I dream things that never were and I say, "Why not?"

—*George Bernard Shaw*

Dreams and poetry are the crown jewels of our imagination, springing from the creative unconscious and touching our originality, aliveness, and unknowable self. And whether a dream is a poem or a poem is a dream really depends on where you choose to enter the circle.

Some poems begin in us as children, long before we are able to speak, and even longer before we have the ability to write a word. Then, when ready, an unexpected gift arrives.

A writer once told me the dream is the most perfect story because it is all unconscious. It captures the unthinkable, uninhibited newness, and vivid images.

In this chapter, poets pull their dreams from a place of timelessness. Sometimes they write in a hypnogogic state—between awake and sleep—that dreamy state between our conscious and unconscious, the land where images, feelings, and reveries glide through, waiting to be caught.

Dreams offer us transcendence. Vincent van Gogh said, "I dream my painting and then paint my dreams."

Just when we think a dream is forever fixed in our memory, in a flash the dream can vanish. A great example of the fleeting power of the dream as poetry can be seen in the work of the nineteenth-century romantic poet, Samuel Taylor Coleridge. Among his finest lyric poems is *Kubla Khan*. Coleridge awoke from a dream with a vision of a place like Xanadu, the summer palace of the emperor of China. He immediately wrote the first few hundred lines that he vividly recalled. Unfortunately, he was interrupted by a visitor from another town. And when Coleridge returned to his poem an hour later, the remaining 200 to 300 lines had vaporized, and were lost forever. However, what remained has become one of the greatest romantic poems in the English language. One can only wonder what might have been written if the visitor had not stopped by that day.

The following dreams share poetic visions, and fresh metaphors as individual as a fingerprint. Readers are invited into the most private places of someone else's soul.

* * *

LOU REED IS DEAD
SUSAN OBRECHT, LCSW

Lou Reed was a member of the Velvet Underground and wrote Walk on the Wild Side. *In his wild days, he swung sexually both ways and hung out with David Bowie and Andy Warhol. In his later years, he married Laurie Anderson. By that time, he lived in the West Village. He began following Buddhism and a more serene lifestyle. A liver transplant went wrong and he died in October, 2013.*

Memorial to be held
At their Victorian beach house.
Expansive yellow exteriors.
Cerulean blue trim
Languid blonde models pose-lounge on the vast porch.

I turn to see my husband rushing down a grey city sidewalk
The flowers I requested in hand.
Sharp focus on crimson marigold.
Head snapped
Dangles.

Hurry, instead, to a greenhouse
(grateful, my beloved, for your indulgence).
Choose a pot of ivies
To plant in the widow's back garden.

We return to a final rite.
Lou's ashes steeping in a teapot.
As the smoke drifts up into the bright sky
Our circle breathes deep
To take in
a little bit
of him.

Susan Obrecht, LCSW, is training analyst, supervisor, and faculty member at the National Institute for the Psychotherapies and the Manhattan Institute for Psychoanalysis. Susan loves introducing students to the complexities and pleasures of working with dreams. She has a private practice in New York City.

NIGHT VISION
SUSAN HANS, PhD

I wrote this a number of years ago. My dream was interrupted by some crazy weather, obviously a harbinger of more to come. I was at my house in East Hampton, which was surrounded by wonderful old oaks. Having sold it in 2008, I miss it a lot and have since heard that the folks who bought the house cut down many of the trees because of their messy sap and leaves; you know—life …

The trees keep me awake
Old oaks wild with the wind
Echo the afternoon ocean's roar
High above my room

Shades banging against the panes
Interrupt soft dreams of bygone loves
Sight can pretend the night is still
Yet insistent sound screams nature's tantrum—
Look at me, look at me!

Pulling the tattered cord down
Expecting dark roiling clouds
To obscure the almost full moon
In such a noisy woods

But stars surprise my eyes
Trees scratch the spangled sky
Tornado on earth, heavenly peace above
The crazed contrast banishes sleep

Susan Hans, PhD, is a psychologist/psychoanalyst and supervisor in private practice in New York City. She cites her poetry "career" as stemming from the third grade when she penned her first work, "Bonnie and Her Dog." In more recent years, the creative inspiration she finds for her poems and songs often comes to her in the form of dreams or reveries.

PSYCHOANALYSIS: A DREAM
VICTORIA POLLOCK, MA

I had this dream about me and my analyst. It's disguised as an erotic poem about my analysis. I think it's about feeling that psychoanalytic intimacy is transgressive. In the dream there is the thrill of wrongdoing. However, what I find really thrilling is working closely together, shoulder to shoulder, head to head, and somehow penetrating each other in ways that feel out of control and ecstatically wrong, but are, in fact, right.

> They are sitting on the floor,
> They lean hard against each other.
> Studying the cell phone,
> Too close,
> Transgressive,
> Their bodies crash together, side by side,
> as if it's not happening at all, but it is.
> Longing, balled up tight like paper
> tossed in a trash can, unfolding.
> They are falling into and through each other
> with everything they've got.

Victoria Pollock, MA, RSW, RMFT, Toronto, Canada, is a psychoanalyst and psychotherapist in private practice and is an adjunct faculty member at the School of Theology at the University of Toronto. She writes, "On Tuesdays I sing and dance and talk to people at the soup kitchen; as far as I know, nobody minds."

SENESCENCE
ALEXANDRA EITEL, LP

The setting of this dream is my father's house in northern New Hampshire. In the dream appears the middle-aged father of my adolescence shortly before his divorce from my mother, and the young man he once was whom I've never met.

The young man who resembles you
opening a door in my father's house
half built, as I am—
dear God I want you to know that
you stand in the living room
watching the fire burn itself out

I remember the best day of your life
you were in love, you were a saint
you were almost word for word forever
you walked straight and tall against the storm and hollow
your love left
when she left

on our backs looking at stars, sprays of light
Rachmaninov,
the old loved landscape
fading from the window
saying, in your voice,
come back.

Alexandra Eitel, MFA, LP, is a psychoanalyst in private practice in Manhattan. She completed her psychoanalytic training at the National Institute for the Psychotherapies and is associate editor of *Psychoanalytic Perspectives*.

THE MERMAID'S TALE
LEANNE DOMASH, PhD

When I saw the call for submission of poems from dreams, I was inspired. These are my two favorite formats. Poems and dreams can transform. This poem expresses diving deeply into love, into friendship, and into the unconscious. I hope the reader, if only fleetingly, can experience the joy and pleasure of the young woman in love, the warmth of the woman laughing with her close friends and children, and the anticipation and lightness of the mermaid diving into the unknown.

We are all in a hotel lobby.

"You don't know how serious we are.
We are deep," the glamorous woman told me,
describing her relationship with her boyfriend.

Then I see another woman, Mexican, laughing,
slapping a child good-naturedly,
talking with women friends,
her arms moving like an octopus.

Then I, naked from the waist up,
and having grown a mermaid tail,
glide through the lobby as if propelled by a motor
The watery air carrying me right up to the front desk.

Free, light, settling.
Ready for my swim.

Leanne Domash, PhD, has completed an intensive training program at the Los Angeles Embodied Imagination Institute, a post-Jungian course of dream study developed by Robert Bosnak. This work facilitates creativity and change. She is in private practice in Manhattan and is consultant, NYU Postdoctoral Program in Psychotherapy and Psychoanalysis, and voluntary psychologist, Mt. Sinai Beth Israel Medical Center.

THE NEXT STOP
PAULINE NOLAN

From a dream I had in 2011. I wrote this poem in one sitting waiting to go into a counseling session. I was going to rewrite it and improve the rhythm but decided to leave it raw. This dream is still very vivid in my mind years after I dreamt it.

I met the love of my life in India in 2006. He proposed in 2007 and we fought hard to get him to Australia. He didn't make it and was married off by his family in 2010. We are still very connected. Writing this poem turned out to be a healing process for me. When the proofs arrived, I woke up the next morning knowing I was free. I still felt warmly to my ex-fiancé, but the painful pining had gone. It was an unexpected relief.

A clearing in the jungle
Great green leaves jammed in together
In canopies and arches mangled
And dripping with steamy weather

Brown dirt oval shaped
And there he was on a chair
Red angry faces half-baked
Why is he still sitting there?

I am on a train
Stopped at the scene
He turns, twists and strains
Trying to be seen

The train is leaving now
I say: Hurry and get on board
I can't, with furrowed brow
I have to face this hoard

I want to darling, really
But this is a family trial
Everyone is angry
I'll come in a little while

The judge was then presiding
Her father has much wealth
Relatives are blaming him
Him for her poor health

I'm sorry my darling, so sorry
I really had no choice
I look at you and worry
In this I had no voice

My family and her blame me
Now she says divorce
She has lost her baby
Life will take its course

The train moves out, I'm waving
Tears in both our eyes
Both our hearts are aching
Their accusations fly

Next stop there are children
I step off into a field
Covered with round stones of green
So that the sick are healed

Now I hold him as a child
His dark hair, face content
I look softly down and smile
All his tears are spent

Bending down I pick up
A cool green smooth round stone
His little hand is cupped
To hold it as his own

The court scene flashes
Everyone is drunk
Red and angry faces
He's in his prison bunk

I hold him as an infant
That part he sent with me
The one in court just can't
Continue, breathe or be

Will he get the next train
Once he's faced his fate?
Or do I travel on again
And will it be too late?

And what of the infant man
Placed in my tender care
The green stones held tightly in his hand
It's more than I can bear.

Pauline Nolan is a psychologist in Australia with many interests: woodcarving, swimming, watercolors, writing, bookbinding, cooking, sailing, kung fu. She is by nature very adventurous and will take on any new thing that draws her. It never used to be that way, always wishing and hoping, but life is different now.

THE LOST SHOES
LINDA SIEGEL, MPS

This poem was inspired by my work with a patient whose sessions evoked powerful images and feelings of longing to write and dream.

She lost her shoes every day.
Well, she didn't really lose them, they just got lost.
In the rubble of other lost shoes,
and incomplete pairs of shoes
each morning her father dug through
and pulled a pair
A matching pair usually, but an unmatched pair occasionally.
The pink ones, or one pink one, and one orange one, were happily secured.
And whether or not they matched her dress,
the insignificance of what any part of her outfit looked like,
she felt found
because her father found her shoes for her so that she could go to school, and walk on her feet and be a whole person in the world
Except, every day, at 12 noon when she wasn't sure if her mom was still real
She walked to the principal's office in the shoes her father found for her that morning
and called her mom
To hear her voice and to remember that her mom existed and thus, so did she
for the remainder of the day
Until she got home from school and remembered that she couldn't find anything
Especially her real mom.

Linda Siegel, MPS, ATR-BC, LCAT, is an art psychotherapist in Brooklyn and a tenured professor at Pratt Institute. She has taught art therapy in the Dominican Republic, Chile, and Argentina. She works with children, adolescents, and parent/infant diads, and has extensive training in couples therapy. She is an artist who has recently enjoyed making medicine dolls.

CHAPTER TWO

From image to words: one unconscious speaks to another

Seven psychoanalysts were invited to respond to a range of surrealist paintings—including works by Picasso, Dali, Giacometti, Magritte, Max Ernst, and Jackson Pollock. The respondents were asked to select an image that provoked an unconscious response and to put that response into words: from one sensory modality to another, one unconscious speaking to another.

Influenced by Freud, the surrealists seized the elusive unconscious. Their works often contained elements of surprise, unexpected fun, and disturbing juxtapositions. They disdained literal meanings, but rather looked for undertones, very much like psychoanalysts.

During the 1920s when surrealism flourished, a sign hung on André Breton's bedroom door while he was sleeping: "Do not disturb, artist at work." The young poet saw surrealism as a revolutionary movement that would liberate the imagination and eliminate the effect of reason.

As for Dali, in his studio in Cadaques, he would sit holding a paintbrush dangling over a metal pail. The instant he'd fall asleep the brush would clatter into the pail and awaken him from his dreamlike state. Then he would paint disjointed images directly from his unconscious. Dali said, "There is only one difference between a madman and me. I am not mad."

A Dali graphite drawing inspired Gilbert Cole. Galit Atlas chose a moody work by Picasso. Warren Wilner had a humorous take on a Max Ernst painting. Robert Stolorow and Julia Schwartz joined together in the creative process, inspired by a Giacometti sculpture. Spyros Orfanos selected Picasso's iconic and emotionally powerful painting *Guernica*, which was issued as a commemorative stamp in Spain. Philip Ringstrom wrote about how a Jackson Pollock painting changed his artistic vision. And from Australia, Colette Rayment responded to a Magritte painting of a reverse mermaid.

* * *

Picasso, *Sleeping Woman with Shutters*, 1936, oil on canvas.

FIREWORKS
GALIT ATLAS, PhD

When we got home Mom was already in bed. She said she didn't feel well and asked that we not bother her. Dad went into his study, and I opened the door to the bedroom and watched her sleeping. I got close and whispered in her ear, "Mom, can I sleep next to you?" She didn't answer and I got in on Dad's side of the bed, covered myself with the blanket and watched her. "Mom, we saw fireworks," I whispered. She opened an eye and smiled at me, "Good, I'm glad you had a good time," and immediately shut her eyes again—before I had a chance to tell her that I actually did not have such a good time and that I don't like fireworks at all.

Galit Atlas, PhD, is a psychoanalyst and clinical supervisor in private practice in Manhattan. Atlas is the author of *The Enigma of Desire: Sex, Longing and Belonging in Psychoanalysis*. She is on the faculty at NYU Postdoctoral Program in Psychotherapy and Psychoanalysis and at the National Institute for the Psychotherapies. Atlas is a contributor to *The New York Times*, and writes essays elucidating psychoanalysis for the general public.

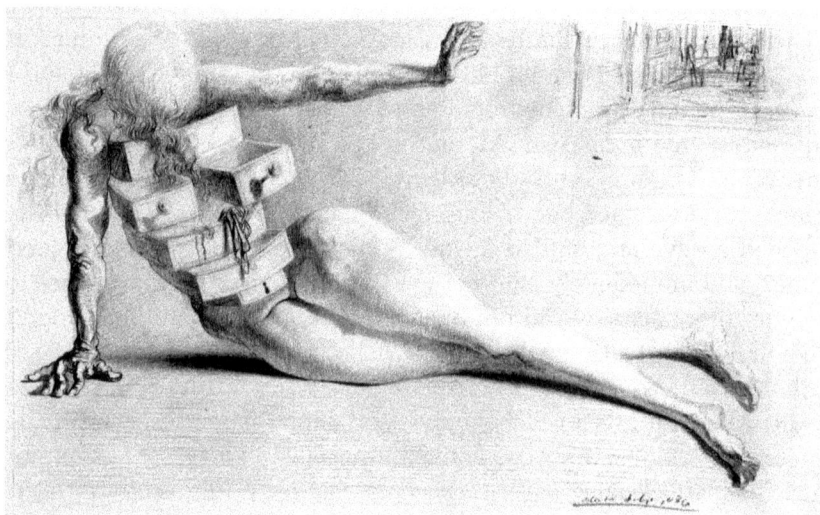

Salvador Dali, *City of Drawers*, 1936, ink on paper.

TERRIBLE GENEROUS BEAUTY
GILBERT W. COLE, PhD

No, it wasn't thieves, it wasn't rapacious marauders, and it wasn't the malevolence of another. Alas, no. If it had been, perhaps then this sorry state would be so much easier to bear. It was I—or rather it was, I was going to say, my acquiescence, but that is not sufficient. It was my generosity. Yes, my generosity. Beauty comes with its costs, its responsibilities. I am so beautiful. Still. I know it. Just look upon me. Please do not think that I wish to exaggerate my condition. Or to complain. I do not wish to add to the keening of the general world. Can you tell me, why can't they be quieted? Why can't they be soothed? But you asked, and so I answer. Gladly. I am so beautiful that it was simply wrong to be stingy. I could not bear to be stingy. I presented myself to you all. Here, take me; take my beauty if it pleases you. Oh, how it pleased you all. How it pleased me that you wished to take. To be perfectly honest, it pleased me greatly to be ransacked by the—how shall I put it—by the hungriest of you. My most ardent lovers. Hungrily feeding. Hungrily reaching for more of me. Here, take, I offer you all.

Gilbert W. Cole, PhD, LCSW, is the author of *Infecting the Treatment: Being an HIV Positive Analyst* (The Analytic Press, 2002) and *Fortune's Bastard, or Love's Pains Recounted*, a novel (Chelsea Station Editions, 2013). He is in private practice in New York City.

Max Ernst, *Euclid*, 1945, oil on canvas.

SIR REAL

WARREN WILNER, PhD

Ah! Sir Real
Strange, eponymous defender of the Real
Champion of surrealing our Real concealing
With eyes made surreal by Surreal-eye-zing our Realing
Sir Real.

Images of light and dark, real and surreal combine in seamless
union as in film Reel
Seen in assuring light, while avoiding Real-eye-zing surreal
night.

Mercurial and terrifying phantasms of surreal and real, dark
and light fill Sir Real's sight
By keeping us in the light he protects from all but brief glimpses
of this terrible sight.
Every night must have its light
Sir Real, our knightlight.

Furtive efforts to escape the surreal by our own Idealing
Just another Real concealing
From which we are flung Realing
While Sir Real continues his surrealing.

Now trying to Surreal our own Realing
But can there be Real Surrealing,
While the Real continues its concealing.

Finally Un-Realing
We attempt Sir Real's mask lifting
To leave no Real left for him to surreal
Surreal and Real eyes now closing in the Un-Real.

Having now no one to bring us our light
And Sir Real his night
Throws us into terrible fright, from which we try to take flight
We replace Sir Real's mask that, again, also permits us Real
concealing, and Sir Real, once more, his surrealing.

Who is Sir Real?
Is he Real?
Our lone, masked knight.

Warren Wilner, PhD, is in private practice in New York City. He is a training, supervising analyst, and faculty member, William Alanson White Institute; and faculty member and supervisor, Postdoctoral Program of New York University. He has published more than twenty papers, a major theme being working from immediate and direct experience in psychoanalytic psychotherapy.

René Magritte, *Collective Invention*, 1934, oil on canvas.

MAID-MER BY THE SEA
COLETTE RAYMENT, PhD

Beached, washed up flotsam or jetsam on the breakers' edge. Dugong with lovely legs and dark unknown regions. Smelly? Slimy? Smooth or silky? Can't say.

Enigma, I want to marvel at you.

Dorsal punk! Hybrid freak! I loathe you because you tease me out of mind. Out of body more likely. And aren't those knees, on inspection, quite the knobbly sort?

My head is smothered in your fish body and my belly bloated with the small fish you eat. My legs and feet lack the finny something you ought to have and I am no more than a mermaid in reverse.

Brave sturgeon from the northern seas? White bait amplified. Can I dive with you or lie here sunning myself in the surf? Oxymoron! How dare you confuse me landlubber, deep sea diver.

I give up. I can't breathe. I never did enjoy a compromise or composite things. A purist at heart I request you to go back to the deep, trail those lovely legs tail-like behind you and leave me uncomfortable here on the shore.

Or, Frog-prince, nay, Fish-prince remove that finny helmet and morph into something I can understand.

Colette Rayment, PhD, was formerly artistic director of Australian Theatre for Young People and founding president of the Centre for Religion, Literature and the Arts, University of Sydney. She is in private practice and writes to explore psychoanalytic and literary understandings of transformative experience. She presented on "Aboriginal Painting and Trauma" at the World Congress for Psychotherapy in Sydney, 2011.

Jackson Pollock, *Number 1A*, 1948, oil on canvas.

LOVE AT FIRST SIGHT
PHILIP RINGSTROM, PhD

Growing up in the Midwest meant facing constant derision about Jackson Pollock's paintings. "Who couldn't 'squirt' paint all over canvas?" It didn't help that his work was only available on color plate pages of books of modern art where they were flattened into two dimensions when in fact they were painted in three.

In the summer of 1995, I had been painting for a year. It changed how I saw everything, though I never quite realized the degree to which until I rounded a corner in the Hirshhorn Museum in Washington, DC and confronted my first Pollock. It drew me into its tangled web of incomprehensible lines, woven-in patterns only a prejudice free mind could grasp. Gazing at my first Pollock was like falling in love.

Approaching and retreating, viewing from every conceivable angle, newness abounded. Endless squirts and flecks of paint, human detritus like cigarette butts impregnated it—all of which gave rise to an in-your-face surface between you and what becomes its infinite depth.

This was as close as I had ever yet come to staring into the abyss of the artist's unconscious in a manner that spoke directly to mine.

Philip Ringstrom, PhD, is senior training analyst at the Institute of Contemporary Psychoanalysis in Los Angeles. He is on the editorial boards of *Psychoanalytic Dialogues*, *IJPSP*, and *Psychoanalytic Perspectives*, as well as on the board of directors of both ICPSP and IARPP. In addition to sixty professional publications, his book *A Relational Psychoanalytic Approach to Couples Psychotherapy* won the Goethe Award for 2014 in psychoanalysis. He has been drawing, painting, and sculpting for two decades, primarily portraits and human figures.

A stamp printed in Spain circa 1981 of Picasso's *Guernica*, 1937, oil on canvas.

THE RETURN OF GUERNICA
SPYROS D. ORFANOS, PhD

You are not an isolated painting and do not have an isolated story. The blood of your people flowed at 4:30 on a sunny April afternoon in 1937. The skies turn black with aerial bombers. Your paint is dry before the smoke has cleared.

Your creator had the allure of Alexander the Great, paintbrush in hand instead of sword, and dealing with it great blows to the attacks on human dignity by Franco and Hitler and Mussolini. He conceived and enacted you in Paris with astonishing speed on May Day; only six days after the Luftwaffe terrorized the town. Pablo with his urgency preferred artistic detachment when facing his era. You contain multitudes: a mother carrying her dead child, a light bearer, anguished horses and bulls, and a Minotaur with Cretan savagery. Collapse. Agony. Panic. Death.

A small stamp is issued to commemorate your return to Madrid after the demise of Franco. It was the painter's wish that it would be after. It took forty-four years to cease your orphanhood from Spain. But in Guernica, the people still wait for you.

I am under the spell of Pablo. "Worship the virtue of ancestors," he whispers, "not ancestors themselves."

"What triggered your neck problem?" asks the neurosurgeon.

"The Fascists," I answer.

"But there are no Fascists in New York. This is not Casablanca," he says. "You are misinformed," I say.

Spyros D. Orfanos, PhD, ABPP, is clinic director at the New York University Postdoctoral Program in Psychotherapy and Psychoanalysis. He is past president of the International Association of Relational Psychoanalysis and Psychotherapy and the Division of Psychoanalysis of the American Psychological Association. Picasso's *Guernica* is a painting that overwhelms him because of the way it metabolizes one of the great traumas of the twentieth century. The creator balances solitude and solidarity, feeling and action, and his personal history with that of humankind.

Alberto Giacometti, *Walking Man*, 1960, bronze.

INTERPRETING GIACOMETTI
JULIA M. SCHWARTZ, MD and
ROBERT D. STOLOROW, PhD, PhD

The elongated figures typical of Giacometti evoke a feeling of isolation and aloneness, which may evoke grief in us even as we embrace it. The human figure is reduced to its skeletal essence—perhaps to a walking shadow-spirit—and yet is fully grounded, not in collapse. The capacity to embrace fully the vulnerability, tenuousness, and fragility of finite human existing is beautifully conveyed in his works.

These images also seem to concretize the way we think of the analytic process: stripping away intellectual defensive layers in order to find some essential deeper emotional meaning or existential dilemma.

Julia M. Schwartz, MD, and **Robert D. Stolorow**, PhD, PhD, are psychoanalysts practicing in Santa Monica, California. Schwartz is also an artist whose paintings have been exhibited internationally and featured in *New American Paintings*. Stolorow is also a philosopher whose most recent book is *World, Affectivity, Trauma: Heidegger and Post-Cartesian Psychoanalysis*.

CHAPTER THREE

Love calls: a call for love

L ove calls us in the most astonishing and exciting ways. The experience of love often catches us by surprise, from the simplest quiet moment to wildly dramatic delirium. The currents of feeling flow back and forth, lighting up the darkness with intense fire. We get up before dawn and think of the other. Passion sends us into complete euphoria, both terrifying and exhilarating, filling us with intoxication. Love makes us dance, sing, write, paint, laugh, and run wild. And in these incandescent moments we feel most alive.

In response to our call for poetry and short stories, we were flooded with submissions. Contributors ran the gamut from psychoanalysts to new as well as accomplished poets and writers.

The selections in this chapter examine the ecstatic exuberance and delight of pure love, the sensual desire and aching for erotic love, the exhilaration of finding a new chance at love, the heartbreak of losing love; they explore playful love in a wheelbarrow, and cross-species love between a primate and a winged creature: all that illuminates the universality of love.

One poem depicts a therapist who helps a couple fall back in love, and another is a new translation of ancient lyrical verses written by Greek poetess, Sappho, in 600 BCE. Also included are love of one's home, sharing a bed, the athletics of love, and the possible synchronization of two hearts. These are followed by a very short story about an insomniac analyst who awakens in the middle of the night, haunted by midnight fantasies of her husband's betrayal.

* * *

LOVING ELYA
JON PEARSON

To lie in bed like a great boy squid wrapping my arms around a beauti-ful girl squid like Elya is like filling the night sky with my face to the edges of the universe. It is like losing myself in cottonwood, dogwood, rainbows, and peacock hats. Elya gives off a womanly heat that makes me forget about rude neighbors or the falling housing market. The kindness of small things fills me like blood, like some warm memory of warm things.

I should like, now, to go upstairs and wake Elya with guitar music, if only I played the guitar. I would sing in Spanish about the beauty of roses and the long ago death of … of a bird, a tiny yellow bird who died hopelessly against the mighty rocks, and how sad it is. I would sing in Spanish, though I don't speak Spanish. The words would come to me easy as sleep from my man-squid soul, the man-squid that Elya has made of me—the song that Elya has made of me, because now I feel like song, whereas before Elya I was old shoes in a closet, I was pants over a chair, I was a man brushing his teeth alone in a mirror before bed.

Once, I wished to be famous, to be known. Now I just wish to know Elya in ever smaller ways. I wish to know things as simple as water-ing a lawn and remembering to remove the used coffee filter from the coffeemaker because that makes Elya happy. And yesterday I sat with Elya on the steps of our house and held her hand—and it reminded me of all the times I have held her hand, and how the smallness of it seems almost infinite, the softness, the she-ness of it. And how there is no word for "she," no real word for the she that is "her" and only her, that is Elya and no one else, ever. And how small her hand is compared to the big giant world. And a shriek of pleasure ran through me and reminded me of how I have been alone for so many years and how "not alone" now is bigger than any fear, and yet how small her hand is.

Each night, I dance before Elya at the foot of our bed, in my under-pants. I hike them up as high as they will go, and feel sort of bald and chubby and old and ridiculous. But in my belly I feel a happiness too simple to name, an almost idiot delight, as I bob and cavort like an over-sized waterbug. Every morning we kick our legs in the air and make up some random poem about cradle fish or pelicans or fat blue skies—so the day won't take itself too seriously. And every night, for eighteen months, we have kissed good night. She calls me "coconut head," and I call her "raptor girl." It is nice trying to find her beautiful mouth in the dark. Kissing Elya is a sacred, slow thing that grows as it gets smaller. On the other side of that mouth is a woman of such honesty and generosity, such daring and kindness. I kiss her and feel all barefoot and safe, as if I were floating in the soft, ferocious history of love, as if every woman I ever wanted, ever wanted and "couldn't have," were in her mouth, that little cathedral of female of lady of woman of pretty of roses and birds and bees and life eternal.

Jon Pearson is a cartoonist, writer, speaker, and international creative thinking consultant. His short stories have appeared in numerous literary journals. His work has been nominated for a 2014 and 2016 Pushcart Prize. Also, he was once a little boy. And he still believes that love is bigger than fear, and that courage, caring, and creativity can save the world. He lives in Los Angeles and thoroughly loves his now wife, Elya.

* * *

WHEELBARROW
LISA A. JACOBSON

i.   In the beginning there was the wheelbarrow, which they kept in the bedroom and filled with books, fruit, and phone messages.
ii. Later when the sleeplessness got too much, they used it to wheel each other around the house. Once they filled it with soup, which they ladled into bowls and ate with chunks of bread.
iii. The wheelbarrow was silver. It glittered in the dark and made whistling sounds like birdsong. Sometimes it hummed.
iv. Once she pushed him backwards into the wheelbarrow and tossed the book after him, saying: Stay there until you've read the first act of *Hamlet* at least!

Lisa A. Jacobson, from Melbourne, Australia, is the author of *The Asylum Poems* (2016), *South in the World* (2014), *The Sunlit Zone* (2012), and *Hair & Skin & Teeth* (1995). Her work has been internationally awarded and twice shortlisted for the Montreal Poetry Prize. She is a poet, social worker, and dog trainer.

FALLING IN LOVE, COUPLES THERAPY, SESSION ONE
KATHLEEN SULLIVAN, LCSW

again
     strangers
         outside my door
blown
  up the brick walk
     like cardboard
    discarded and torn

from his hardened eye, a tiny fire
         spits
 she
has thin hair and bitten nails

I could never love them

how do you do sit down tell me
your story your story tell me your   story

       soon once more
I see …

she is empty like the dark universe and beautiful and sad
he is a monk tending
earth's fire

closer they are coming closer.
closer.

Kathleen Sullivan, LCSW, MFA. *Mudluscious.* It was this word, famously invented by E. E. Cummings, that opened me as a child to the idea that good language could transform the human experience. It is Cummings I turn to after a half century helping others find language for preverbal experience, forgotten loves, and unspeakable longing: *love is more thicker than forget.*

IF YOU WISH (iPhone Poetry)
JACK LEVIN

To shut me up
Calm me down
Bring me back
To who I was
When you once
Loved me
Take my hand
Draw me near
Hold me close
Keep me still
Or let me be
And see who
I become.

Jack Levin lives in New York City, where he spent more than thirty-five years as a litigator. He is now a domestic and international arbitrator and mediator. In the past sixteen years he has written 1,300 poems in the moment, virtually all on a handheld device, and sent them to friends and acquaintances around the world.

FREEDOM
GOTTFRIED M. HEUER, PhD

A female bonobo,
the smallest of the great apes,
in one of England's zoos
has been observed to accidentally
have caught a starling—
both
are stunned:
the bird in shock, I guess,
the bonobo, it seems,
full of concern and worry
for her little feathery prisoner:
might she have harmed it
unintentionally?!
This
just takes moments—
each heart beating audibly
to the other
then,
with utter, gentle care
she cradles in one hand
the still startled starling
and climbs nimbly
to the highest branch
of the tallest tree within the prison that's her home.
And there,
to gain even greater height,
she wraps both legs around the trunk
to have
both hands free to hold the frightened bird. Then,
with infinite gentleness
of tender, loving care she unfolds its wings, first one, and then
the other, holds one spread wing
in either hand

like an offering, before,
with all her power
in one big arc of movement,
she sends it flying skywards to the sun—
and—
freedom.

Gottfried M. Heuer, PhD, Jungian training-psychoanalyst and-supervisor, neo-Reichian body-psychotherapist, has over thirty-five years of clinical practice in West London. He is an independent scholar with more than seventy published papers; ten congress-proceedings for the International Otto Gross Society; and his books include *Sacral Revolutions* (2010), *Sexual Revolutions* (2011), and *Freud's 'Outstanding' Colleague/Jung's 'Twin Brother': Otto Gross* (2016). He is also a published graphic artist, photographer, sculptor, and poet.

I BEG YOU, GONGYLA
SAPPHO (630–570 BCE)
TRANSLATED BY SPYROS D. ORFANOS, PhD

Before the era of luminous rationalism the Classical Greeks idealized beauty and Eros. Sappho, the poet from the Aegean island of Lesbos, best exemplified this sensibility with her pure lyricism, full of Dionysian impulses and dynamism. For twenty-five centuries her love poems have survived, albeit in fragments, because they affirm the senses.

Come back again, I beg you, Gongyla.
Reveal yourself in your garment
white as milk; o what desire
forever around you, my lovely girl.

This charming garment stirs her
who beholds you, for she who expresses
this reproach to you is the goddess herself
Cyprus-born, whom now I invoke.

Spyros D. Orfanos, PhD, ABPP, is clinic director at the New York University Postdoctoral Program in Psychotherapy and Psychoanalysis. He is past president of the International Association of Relational Psychoanalysis and Psychotherapy and the Division of Psychoanalysis of the American Psychological Association. He studies art, literature, and philosophy as aspects of the whole human endeavor, often called civilization and culture, but not as social scientists use the terms. He claims to be able to hear Sappho singing *Eros, Eros, Eros.*

I WANT TO GO HOME

RACHEL AMEY

I want to go home
Where the light is lower on me
with a smell of pipe smoke
and expectancy
The soft comfort of loss
Envelops me
With its slow sweet fumes

I want to go home
Where the background clock
Counts the hours for me
The pleated lampshade
Shades the fire from me
And condensation creeps
From the corners of the pane

I want to go home
Where the warm stale air
Hangs like kindness in the hall
And unremarkable, unannounced
Your hand on the handle
You open the door,
Your face relaxed in the frame.

Rachel Amey is based in Edinburgh, Scotland. Rachel's recent poetry includes her solo performance piece, "Where have I come from? Where are we going?" Her next work will be "I've lost the lies I told myself." She collaborates on new writing projects, is published in anthologies, and has received commissions for her work.

OTHER HALF
ZOIE KENNEDY

With you away I treat myself
to your half of the bed;
stretch to feel the space (within myself)
which has been so full of you
I did not recognize it as mine.

I am bigger than I thought.

On this side you have left the trace
of your regard for me.

On this side I am fuller, stronger,
more certain and peaceful.

And the space is not empty,
but filled
with love.

With so much of me here,
no wonder I felt emptied.

So, with you away, I will treat myself
to your half of the bed,
bathe happily in the space,
and know that I am loved.

Zoie Kennedy is a British actress, poet, director, artist, producer, writer, and founder of *Twice Shy Theatre*. She has embarked on her most ambitious creative project to date … motherhood!

TASKS/ATHLETE
PAUL OERTEL, MFA

I am

running
jumping
throwing
turning
leaping
hopping
rolling
crawling
kneeling
leaning
bending
twisting
pushing
hurdling
wriggling
pulling
lifting
reaching
spinning
extending
grasping
holding
rotating
skipping falling rising stepping stooping bounding springing
descending prancing torquing
striding strutting climbing folding twirling stretching sliding
spiraling diving orbiting ascending

because I love you

Paul Oertel, MFA, lives in southwestern France. He is a dancer, singer, actor who has performed internationally for over forty years. Artistic research, making dance videos, Jin Shin Jyutsu, and organic gardening are the focus of his life at his home where he lives with his creative life partner, choreographer Nancy Spanier. This poem is from a series called *Love Poems*, fifty poems of fifty words, each written during his fiftieth year.

HEART SHOCK
ALICE HAYWARD

We were to be at the hospital at eight.
What if this were our last time together?
There was too much unsaid between us
to start to say it now.

They were going to stop his heart,
make it stand still,
just as I longed to do the moment we met.
The doctor was going to shock it,
in hopes of giving it a regular rhythm.

His body was lost in the hospital bed.
He seemed to have shrunk.
His individuality erased
by the folds of the thermal blanket.

He was afraid.
I was afraid for him.
Afraid I could lose him one way or another.
It broke my heart.

At four o'clock, he had the procedure.
At six we left.
We drove down clogged freeways
happy his heart had a regular beat.
I longed for a procedure
to get our hearts to beat as one.

Alice Hayward lives, loves, paints, and writes in Los Angeles, California. She's published poems and short stories as well as lectured internationally on the development of intelligence and creativity and contributed to professional journals and textbooks in that area. Her paintings are shown in Mexico and the United States.

LOVE IN THE MIDWAY
MARCIA STEINBERG, PsyD

Julie had another night of insomnia. The husband, Peter, did he love her? Was he carrying on an affair? Was it Lisa, the one with the saluting tits who loved to laugh and enchant the world with a wisecrack and a smile? Earlier that evening Julie spied Lisa and Peter huddled together at the party serenading each other with jokes that Julie couldn't decode. Was Lisa a friend/foe? No matter, Julie knew that Lisa was a questionable comrade at best, a plumed snake charmer in Armani.

As Julie rehearsed images of Peter and Lisa, she concocted a poster gallery of sweaty thighs, spilled wine, sloppy sheets, coiled underwear, whips, and latex.

Increasingly, vivid fantasies of deception cannonballed Julie into orbit. She shimmied out of bed and tiptoed into Peter's office. Being a husband stalker of reliable skill, Julie was hell-bent on finding proof of betrayal. Some small sliver of sanity within Julie admonished her for this transgression. Hadn't she quit these nightly rampages?

Julie mowed through Peter's desk. She systematically examined the pockets of Peter's jacket, picked open locked drawers, and finally, dove into the wallet, BlackBerry, and PC. Every rock was unturned, patted, and sniffed. But in the end, Julie felt a bitter comedown. There were no Viagra pills or condoms in the wallet, no indictable texts or emails, no questionable credit card bills … just nothing at all.

Julie took a long, slow walk down the hallway to the kitchen where she poured a glass of cognac, and eyed the stable of anti-anxiety meds lined up on the counter. Downing the elixir of alcohol and Xanax, Julie felt sleepy for the first time that night. There was relief in knowing that the earth's rotation would take her to morning where the day would lead her to the place where love just simply resumes.

Marcia Steinberg, PsyD, LCSW, is a training and supervising analyst at the Institute of Contemporary Psychoanalysis in Los Angeles, and is in private practice in Encino, California. In her spare time she enjoys gardening and decorating her backyard, the results of which have been described as "Beatrix Potter meets House of Wax."

CHAPTER FOUR

Creativity and madness

T he creative insane have always been objects of fascination. One can get close to the edge and then pass to the other side. Aristotle said that no great genius has ever existed without some touch of madness. Madness. What is it? Can it be categorized according to the DSM-5? Is it craziness, oddness, abnormality, a loss of contact with reality, unsound, or an unhinged and darkened mind? What about when someone's a bit nutty or daft? Or is madness the same as psychosis?

We associate so many adjectives, ideas, and characters with lunacy, including brilliance, creativity, and artistic expression. There's the imago of a raving lunatic, the Madwoman of Chaillot, and the lunatic asylum at Charenton from *Marat/Sade*. Madman or genius? Sometimes a fine line separates the two, but where do we make the distinction?

"Is there a single individual in the whole of humanity free from some form of insanity?" asked Erasmus in the sixteenth century. He noted that a man who sees a gourd and takes it for his wife is called insane because this happens to very few people. Mark Twain expressed a similar sentiment when he said, "Let us consider that we are all partially insane; it will unriddle many riddles."

Does a writer aspire to madness? Am I a lunatic too? Can madness make for us, as John Milton says, a heaven of hell or a hell of heaven? Is madness a breakdown or a breakthrough? Shakespeare's eccentric King Lear, his voice raging into the wind, calls out, "O let me not be mad, not mad, sweet heaven!" And yet he is. Hamlet asks, "What is it to be nothing else but mad?"

Many artists who have been touched by such madness have felt their minds were under attack: Lord Byron, Alfred Tennyson, F. Scott Fitzgerald, Anne Sexton. Nietzsche believed that mentally ill poets would have an honored shaman status in simpler times. Robert Lowell, a manic-depressive (now called "bipolar"), moved in and out of McLean Hospital, Harvard's elite psychiatric clinic. Virginia Woolf, in her overwhelming depression, stuffed rocks in her pocket and walked out into the sea. William Stryon, caught in a life-threatening suicidal depression, tells us about his personal descent in his deeply moving and painful narrative, *Darkness Visible: A Memoir of Madness*. In Kate Redfield Jamison's book, *Touched by Fire*, she shows how many creative people are bipolar and suggests a relationship between madness and artistic creativity.

In this chapter, Jim Klein, who is bipolar, offers poetry he wrote while in and out of mental hospitals. "Writing is the most powerful therapy," he says. Also included are excerpts from "Fragments of Madness," an article he wrote that provides a glimpse into his bipolar mind. Klein had his first breakdown at twenty-nine and has since been hospitalized more than twenty times, twice at Greystone, the now abandoned "lunatic asylum" in New Jersey which once held 7,000 disturbed patients.

Klein received his doctorate in English, and was a professor at an East Coast university until he was asked to leave due to a manic episode. He is presently working on a book of poetry, *The Pre-Embroidered Mind*, in which he provides a glimpse of what it's like to live within a bipolar world. "People have very little understanding of what goes on inside the mind as one is going crazy," he says. Klein writes about just such moments—taking the reader inside the experience as it happens to him. He writes and he writes and he writes while a strange story plays out inside his mind. For Jim, "The great breakthrough was understanding *the way* I went crazy. I was trapped in language, the experience being so powerful that it pushed me over the edge and sent me to the hospital."

* * *

5 POEMS AND *FRAGMENTS OF MADNESS*
JIM KLEIN, PhD

TWO ORDERLIES

Two orderlies,
matched, black

Judas goats, in white,
lead two deputies

holding hands
with a woman

and two nurses
with syringes

in a procession
to the Quiet Room.

THIS ROOMMATE THEY HAVE BEDDED ME BY

They have closed against us softly
the darkness of this bare room.
I can hear his heavy breathing,
breathing in some purpose perhaps.
This roommate they have bedded me by
might kill me, I fear.

I send my name into the night.
The handshake explodes greetings in us.
He likes the sound of my ideas,
my refusal of white sheets.
They should all go make house calls
and leave us in peace.

META-BALLS

You watched me
sitting up every night
with tape and Styrofoam balls.
It was six or seven meta-balls
I woke you up with,
at 4:30 a.m., for example,
knowing it was right
because you loved me.

And you were so shrewd,
watching me, listening
to me, and little by little
teaching me to stand
still without rocking,
to swing my arms
naturally, to pitch
my voice lower,
to enunciate.

BLUE SHIPS ON THE WALLPAPER

I'm in my friend's car explaining
a kind of literary physics only
I know how to do and this
plainclothes individual with
his eyes dilated somehow
knocks on the car window—
Can you help me? I'm losing it—
I see it's true, so I tell him,
Get in, take my place,
put your head down
between your knees,
and then, at some point,
he and I change places
and I'm in a straitjacket,
then a yellow ambulance,
and not missing a beat
I'm praising them because
it's not red, explaining
how it should be decorated,
a little boy's room, not
a utility room, blue ships
on the wallpaper.

DADDY

Once I swallowed
a double handful of lithium
because my best friend asked me to.
He borrowed a fifth of vodka
from my landlord
and drank it himself.
My wife leaned on him.
I went into my daughter's room
and laid down with her
in her narrow bed
and called her mommy.
She said Daddy in her sleep.
Her thin arm
was around my neck,
and I wondered if
all the lithium
would kill me.

FRAGMENTS OF MADNESS

The following excerpts are from Jim Klein's article, "Out of Mere Words," the college English title for the original, "Lotts, Horse Piss, and Rotted Straw," published in the James Joyce Quarterly, *Spring, 1976.*

A few years ago I formed the belief I had never understood James Joyce's *A Portrait of the Artist as a Young Man* until I had gone crazy because at the time I was fighting against a ringing in my ears, a shortening field of vision, dizziness, and a wild fear of death. "Lotts," I remembered. "This is the smell of horse piss and rotted straw," I remembered and instantly I threw it into the battle.

This is a wall. That is a window. That is a light switch. I am leaning against a window ledge. This is a bed. I am lying down on the bed. I am going to be all right. I had "talked" to myself. I had saved myself with my own story about myself. At another time, I put into words to myself that I was eating a brownie, and the thought darted after, a sane thought, that no man ever died of eating a brownie, and another, that no man ever committed suicide laughing at himself.

My sickness had consisted in becoming so divorced from my life story that I had ceased to be myself, and even characters like my wife and child had begun to be fictional.

My body had been slowed to an ooze by valium and thorazine but my mind was still spinning. It seemed as if my mind and body were becoming detached and I would float away.

When I was admitted, I feared the "mental patients" with whom I'd be forced to live. To guard against the great irony of being murdered by a crazy man just when I made a personal breakthrough, I introduced myself to my roommate, Dennis, and shared my happy story with him: we were sane and everyone else was crazy. "That's what I've been looking for," Dennis answered.

The radio became very important to me. Because I was unable to sleep, I attempted to find a substitute for sleep that would balance my senses. I blindfolded myself and lay for hours with a portable radio playing on my chest. While this was probably not very smart, it wasn't insane. Yet it looked insane. One of the difficulties with being mentally ill is that one is placed under pressures which are incomprehensible to those who are not ill.

I would pick each word carefully, articulating it fully, speaking in a modulated voice, and watching my auditors to see what effect I was having on them. I practiced pitching my voice low and forming each word as perfectly as I was able. My wife corrected my mistakes. I had to literally learn to speak again. One day, after repeating a particularly mellifluous phrase, I asked her if I was developing a particularly pleasing voice, and she answered that I was beginning to speak in the voice I had spoken in before I became sick.

I also had to learn to walk again. During my illness it became impossible for me to stand still. I unconsciously balanced on my insteps and rocked from side to side. I walked with mechanical stiffness. When I began to get my speech under control, my wife pointed out my eccentric body movement and began a regimen designed to teach me to stand, sit, and walk normally.

When I was going crazy, most people encouraged me to keep talking about my ideas. I was relieved when someone told me to shut up.

It seems to me that mental patients are given handicrafts rather than pen and pencil or books to occupy them. They have gotten ill in a world of words; it is only through words that they can become well again. In this process, the written word is superior to the spoken word. How much transitional volleying is babel? On the other hand, the sick first draft can be edited and rewritten mercilessly until it gradually becomes something true, and unique, and real.

Writing has always seemed magical to me. When I was a child, I was fascinated by blank paper. A stack of clean white paper was an image of infinite possibility. I assembled a large collection of pens and mechanical pencils. After my illness, writing still seemed magical to me, but magical in a different way. To use a crude metaphor, I was outside the magic box rather than inside it.

Dying isn't an art, living is, and art is a way to live, not die.

Jim Klein, PhD, is the author of *Blue Chevies*, *To Eat Is Human Digest Divine*, and *Trinis Talk Like the Birds*, a chapbook. He has published more than 100 poems in literary magazines, including *Beloit Poetry Journal*, *Berkeley Poetry Review*, *Field*, *Gandhabba*, *Onthebus*, *Poetry Now*, *Pulpsmith*, *Unmuzzled Ox*, and many times in the *Wormwood Review*. He was a semi-finalist in the Anthony Hecht Prize, WayWiser Press, London, and the Sawtooth Poetry Prize, Ahsahta Press. He leads a weekly poetry workshop in Rutherford, New Jersey, and edits *The Rutherford Red Wheelbarrow*.

CHAPTER FIVE

The art of Thomas Ogden

Thomas Ogden, a psychoanalyst in San Francisco, is among the most creative analysts practicing today. For him, psychoanalysis is an art and he uses poetry and writing as part of the analytic process. He suggests that we turn to both poetry and psychoanalysis with the hope of reclaiming human aliveness.

Recently Ogden has written two novels: *The Hands of Gravity and Chance* and *The Parts Left Out*. For him, writing is an essential part of life. "I always want to be in the process of writing, it enlivens me. When I'm not writing, I feel a tension in me. When I can't think of anything to write, I write anything—a sentence, an idea I cut out from a previous paper. Until I get past a certain point, I think of myself *not* as a writer, but as one who used to be a writer, or who will be a writer one day; but right now I'm not a writer. Until my writing goes out into the world, I guard it. I don't want input from anyone. What interests me is not what we know, but what we don't know. And sometimes we don't have the words yet or the mind to conceive it. Often I write twenty handwritten pages to yield a good sentence or paragraph. I can't be afraid of wasting time, because productive time couldn't happen without it. I create a state of mind. I live it and breathe it when I'm writing. The work suffuses me. If I get stuck,

I wait until I fall asleep and then the answer occurs to me. When I wake up, I write it down. I know then that the process has taken hold."

I had asked him what is the difference for him between writing analytically and writing fiction and were there any surprises. "I find that writing a novel is a far more difficult form of writing than writing a psychoanalytic essay. In the clinical parts of the latter, there are two figures that are engaged in a form of conversation in which both are changed. In writing fiction, there are four or five characters, the narrator, and the writer who are all talking at the same time. It's a virtual storm of possibility, including the strong possibility that it will come to nothing, which makes me wonder why I'm subjecting myself to this form of experience. The answer is clear: I love the use of language whether spoken between people or as used by a poet, a dramatist, a novelist, or any other form of writer. I would have felt that my life was incomplete if I had not tried my hand at engaging in a form of creativity that I have enjoyed and admired my entire life.

"After writing the first novel, *The Parts Left Out*, I felt that I had only begun to be a novelist and that I would not have genuinely experienced that form of creativity if I did not use what I learned in writing the first novel in my efforts to write a second. The upshot of that feeling was two and a half years of immersion in the writing of *The Hands of Gravity and Chance*. I don't think of the second novel as better than the first, but as more layered. It was far more difficult to write, which isn't always a good sign in writing."

A while ago, Ogden told me a story about Paul Klee that resonated. Klee said that when he was a young painter, his room was filled with ancestors in paint. And over the years, there were fewer and fewer of them. And now it is just him.

In his writings about poems by Frost, Stevens, Heaney, and others, Ogden finds connections between how we listen to poetry and how the therapist listens in the analytic hour. Ogden is interested in what lies between the words of a poem, with particular interest in the sounds and texture of the voice.

In his clinical work, Ogden strives to be receptive to "the music between the notes." He's less interested in the manifest content of the patient's narrative than in the conscious and unconscious feelings that the narrative evokes in him. "In psychoanalysis as in writing, creativity takes place in the exchange between the inarticulate unconscious and the act of thinking, talking, dreaming, writing, and composing. It is like the act of pouring wine into a bottle. Giving that kind of shape to something is the creative act."

Ogden has published twelve books on psychoanalytic theory and practice, which have been translated into nineteen languages. His paper, "The Analytic Third: Working with Intersubjective Clinical Facts," is among the most frequently cited psychoanalytic journal articles by a living author. He was awarded the 2010 Haskell Norman Prize, an international award for "Outstanding Achievement in Psychoanalysis." In 2012 he won the Sigourney Award, an international award for "Significant Contributions to the Field of Psychoanalysis." Two years later, he won the Hans Loewald Award for "An Individual's Distinguished Contribution to Psychoanalytic Education."

Included in this chapter is the first poem that Thomas Ogden published in *Psychoanalytic Perspectives*, as well as a more recent poem. Also included is a poem by his niece, Emily B. Ogden.

* * *

THE KNOT IN THE TEAR
THOMAS OGDEN, MD

When winter darkens the evening sky,
And so much is lost by and by.
Nothing can happen that hasn't before,
A nothing inert to anything more.

I fall deeply into those vacant eyes,
The child I dreamt a future bride.
Fact merely scorns the might have been,
Mocking the promise of soft, soft skin.

What can one say to the sketches of chance,
If no one resists the curtains of dance.
When frankness is cruelty, and kindness a lie,
There is only the silence of words that decry.

Empty chatter suffuses the cool night air,
And tightens still further the knot in the tear.

(*May, 2012*)

CRUMBS
THOMAS OGDEN, MD

The ambulance men arrived,
Four of them.
A lot of times they picked
Her up to take her to the hospital.
This time they were
Bringing her home.

It didn't really bother me that much
Up 'til then—
The radiation and all that—
But this time, outside the house, it did.
It's dumb, but you know what it was
That got me,
It was the crumbs on her lips
And around her mouth and on her gown.
She never would have
Let that happen before—never.
It wasn't her.

I bent down and kissed her
And tasted the cookie crumbs.
I told her I had to run,
I was late for rehearsal.

"Do you want me to drive you?"
She asked. Was she joking?

(December, 1999)

Thomas Ogden, MD, published his debut novel, *The Parts Left Out*, in 2014, and his second novel, *The Hands of Gravity and Chance*, in 2016. He lives in San Francisco where he teaches both psychoanalysis and creative writing.

FOR YOU, TIME
EMILY B. OGDEN, PhD

Your nature forces the memory of her
And I use it as traction
To balance my changes.

I catch her smile in your face
As you swivel in your chair to look at me
And ask what climates I like best.

I want to answer how she would—
To remember her gusty Northwestern persuasion
For hair-whipping winds and sea grass.

I'll teach her to you
If you'll help me remember
How she nodded us forward.

Allow me to sway too far
And bend out of reach because
I know I am rooted in her
for you.

(September, 2004)

Emily B. Ogden, PhD, works as a psychologist in Portland, Oregon. She lives with her husband, son, and two cats.

Handwritten letter by Proust to his mother.

CHAPTER SIX

Letters to Dearest Mother from famous writers

We lay aside a letter never to read it again and at last destroy them out of discretion, so dispense with the most beautiful, the most immediate breath of life.

—Goethe

Dear Reader,

I am writing to you about the magic of letter writing from long ago, an art that has all but vanished—the art of taking pen to paper, and with reflection, capturing innermost thoughts, raw and unedited, then sending them to another.

In this chapter we will read fragments of correspondence by five brilliant authors as they write uncensored letters home to their mothers—speaking eloquently of simple everyday experiences as well as significant emotional moments. The letters reveal the intimate, complex relationships that these literary figures had with their mothers. George Sand responds to her mother's harsh critique of her lifestyle. James Joyce speaks of his "villainous hunger" and the impoverished life of a writer. Flaubert, on a long voyage to the Near East, longs to be united with his mother. Proust writes a midnight letter to his mother sleeping in the next room. Some of the letters are loving, some angry, others disappointed at feeling unseen or unappreciated. Still others cause us to gasp at their audacity. Many of the emotions expressed have the intensity of an analytic session.

Until very recently, a letter writer would send her private thoughts on a time-consuming journey, even if the recipient was relatively close by. A note to a sweetheart, a message easing the worry of another, a chronicle of daily adventures, difficulties, illnesses, challenges, homesickness, or expressions from the heart—all took forever to arrive. Some letters wept, others laughed, or whispered inner secrets. Others professed an undying love, others animosity and anger. Whatever the emotion, letter-writing helped clarify and metabolize feelings. And the writer would often wait weeks or longer for a response.

Oscar Wilde had his own style of mailing his letters. He'd write the letter, stamp the envelope, and throw the letter out his Chelsea window, knowing that some honest passerby would pick up the letter and take it to a mailbox. We know this method worked because many of these letters fetched huge amounts of money at auction years later.

Letters were first written on stone thousands of years ago, pieces of which have been found and translated. Medieval monks copied Greek and Roman letters onto parchment, many of which survived for more than a thousand years, until the Italian Renaissance.

More recently, letters were postmarked, read, and often saved. They might be wrapped with string and put into a trunk in the attic, or stacked in an old shoebox in the back of a closet. Often they were meant to be found by the next generation—fragments of lost narratives—offering secrets, dreams, and heartbreak, glimpses into other parts of the writer's story.

How many letters would never have been written if the authors had easy access to a telephone, or email's universal symbol @. We now have the paperless letter, landing in another computer's inbox (replacing the shoe box), perhaps saved in the Cloud, or deleted into the ether—vanishing as quickly as it was written.

I am deeply grateful to Julie Grenet for the excellent new translations of the letters from George Sand, Flaubert, and Proust. As both a French scholar and a psychoanalyst, Julie brilliantly captures the internal musings of these iconic novelists, allowing us a brief glimpse into their private unedited worlds.

By publishing letters from these great writers, we pay tribute to the lost art of letter writing.

Unconsciously yours,
Bonnie Zindel

* * *

JAMES JOYCE

James Joyce (1882–1941) author of *Portrait of the Artist as a Young Man*, and *Ulysses*, grew up in poverty. He was the oldest of ten children, whose alcoholic father was unable to provide a stable household. As a young man, Joyce was arrogant, aloof, and confident of his genius. His wife Nora said, "I guess the man's a genius, but what a dirty mind he has." After graduating from University College, Dublin, he moved to Paris, where he was unable to shake the poverty that had always plagued him. *Ulysses* (1922) is considered one of the greatest books in the English language. Joyce advanced the use of stream of consciousness and interior monologue, and set the course for a whole new kind of novel.

The letter that follows was written to his mother shortly after he moved to Paris. A month after he sent the letter, he received a telegram from his father: "Mother dying, come home."

Paris, March 20, 1903 (Age 21)

Last month I made up my second month's account and I have reduced my expenses from 161 to 106 francs (hotel bill included)—a reduction that is of 56 francs. My reduction of expenses, however, is accompanied by a lack of clean linen. I have had one handkerchief for three weeks, but I have a grey tie, which is something under a mile in length. It floats all over me so that it is difficult for the world to discover the state of my shirt. One boot is beginning to go. I have taken to wearing my "good" black suit as the "other" is impossible. As for the food I get, I do not always get food, only when I can. Sometimes I take one meal in the day and buy potatoes cooked and dry bread in the street. I do not know if I am getting lean but I can assure you, I have the most villainous hunger. Today I came laughing and singing to myself down the Boulevard Saint-Michel without a care in the world because I felt I was going to have a dinner, my first dinner for three days. I sent in my review of Lady Gregory's book a week ago. I do not know if they put it in the Daily Express: the review was very severe. I am sending two other reviews with this letter.

Last Sunday I went out to the woods of Clamart. I read every day at the Bibiliotheque Nationale and every night at the Bibliotheque Sainte-Genevieve. I never go to the theatre as I have no money. I have no money either to buy books.

I have more than once upset a whole French café by laughing. An old woman shook her umbrella in my face one day—I was laughing so loudly. Come what may, I will lunch tomorrow. You will oblige me very much if you will write to me and tell me what you think of me. I shall read your letter with great anxiety.

Jim

From Gilbert, Stuart (Ed.) (1957). *Letters of James Joyce (Volume 1)*. New York: Viking.

MARGARET FULLER

Margaret Fuller (1810–1850) disappointed her father by being born a girl—and yet he gave his daughter the same education he would have given to a son. As a teenager she was able to speak four languages, and was reading philosophy and literature in those languages. She became the first editor of the transcendentalist journal, *The Dial*, before joining the staff of the *New York Herald* and traveling to Italy as a foreign correspondent. She was the first self-supporting woman journalist in America. She said that Italy brought her back to life—that once she was all intellect and now she was almost all feeling. Her seminal work, *Woman in the Nineteenth Century* was published in 1845, and is considered among the first major feminist works published in the United States. She believed that there is no wholly masculine man and no purely feminine woman. In Rome she met the Marquis Giovanni Angelo Ossoli, who became her lover and later her husband.

This letter to her mother was written just a year after her son, Angelo, was born, and less than a year before she and her family left for the United States. Their ship ran aground near Fire Island, New York, and Fuller, her husband, and child were drowned.

Florence, November 7, 1849 (Age 39)

Dearest Mother,

Of all your endless acts and words of love, never was there any so dear to me as your last letter; so generous, so sweet, so holy! What on earth is so precious as a mother's love; and who has a mother like mine!

It will be sad for me to leave Italy, uncertain of return. Yet when I think of you, beloved mother, of brothers and sisters and many friends, I wish to come.

In the evenings, we have a little fire now; the baby sits on his stool between us. He makes me think how I sat on mine, in the chaise, between you and father. The baby is extremely fond of flowers; he has been enchanted this evening by the splendid gardenia. It seems now as if, with the certainty of a very limited income, we could be so happy! But I suppose if we had it, one of us would die, or the baby. Do not you die, my beloved mother, let us together have some halcyon moments, again, with God, with nature, with sweet childhood, with the remembrance of your trust and good intent; away from perfidy and care, and the blight of noble designs.

From Hudspeth, Robert N. (Ed.) (1987). *Letters of Margaret Fuller*. Ithaca, New York: Cornell.

GEORGE SAND

George Sand (1804–1876) was born Amandine-Aurore Dupin in Paris in 1804, the daughter of a mother who was a bird seller and a father who was the great-grandson of King Augustus II of Poland. Her mother married him a month before George Sand was born. One of the earliest feminists, she lived an independent life in Paris, taking on a man's name and dressing in men's clothing. She justified this by saying that men's clothes were far sturdier and less expensive than the typical dress of a noblewoman at the time. Her male dress allowed her to socialize more freely in a man's world. She championed equality of the sexes. Married at eighteen, she had two children. She and her husband lived apart much of the time and she had other lovers, including Frederic Chopin. She wrote an average of two books a year for more than four decades, and was widely read in her day. Her novels were admired by writers like Balzac, Dostoevsky, and Henry James, and she was an important influence on the Brontës.

In the letter to her mother that follows, she defends her unconventional choices and lifestyle.

May 31, 1831 (Age 27)

[…] You know me rather little, I dare say, my dear mama. It has been many years since we have lived together and often you forget that I am 27 years old and that my character had to have undergone many changes since the time of my youth. In particular, you imagine that I have a love of pleasure, a need for amusement and distractions that I am far from having. It is not crowds, noise, shows and jewels that I need. You alone erroneously think that of me; what I need is freedom. To be all alone on the street and to say to myself, I will dine at 4 o'clock or at 7, if that is my fancy. I'll go to the Tuileries via the Luxembourg Gardens instead of going via the Champs-Elysées, if that is my whim. That is what would please me more than the vapidity of men and the stiltedness of salons. And when I encounter souls who don't understand me at all, who take my innocent fancies for hypocritical vices, I can't be bothered to try to dissuade them […]

My God! What zeal we have here in this world to mutually torment each other, to bitterly reproach each other for our flaws, to pitilessly condemn everything that is not cut to fit our mold […]

You have been told that I was wearing the pants; you've been told wrong. If you were to spend 24 hours here you would see that this is not so. But on the other hand, I do not want a husband who wears my skirts. To each his own clothes, to each his freedom. I have flaws; my husband does too and if I said to you that our marriage is the model marriage, that there has never been a cloud between us, you wouldn't believe it […]

As long as you show me that my presence is enjoyable and that I am dear to you, you will find me happy and grateful. If I find you surrounded by bitter criticisms, offensive suspicions […] I will enjoy the support of my conscience and my freedom. You are too intelligent not to soon realize that I do not deserve all of this harshness. Adieu, dear little mama; my children are doing well […] Write to me, dear mama. I kiss you with all my soul.

Translated by Julie Grenet PhD, LP, from: Lubin, Georges (Ed.) (2013). *Correspondance de George Sand: Édition Critique.* Paris: Classiques Garnier.

GUSTAVE FLAUBERT

Flaubert (1821–1880) was born in Rouen in 1821. He was close to his mother but distant from his father, who scoffed at his literary ambitions. He studied law but hated it, and suffered a nervous breakdown. He turned to writing, and in works such as *Madame Bovary*, he strove to "give prose the rhythm of verse," while writing of ordinary life. He established modern realist narration, with his emphasis on brilliant detail, and his influence is almost too familiar to be visible. He was said to spend hours searching for the perfect word or phrase, and days revising a single page. He never married. As a young man, despite his close ties to his mother, Flaubert embarked on a two-year voyage to the Near East. The last night before his departure he was sobbing on the floor in front of the fire. "I shall never see my mother again! I shall never see my own country again! This journey is too long, too far; it's tempting fate! What madness!" Once on his way, Flaubert wrote to his mother almost every day.

March 24, 1850 (Age 28)

Poor Old Darling,

[...] Sometimes I feel a longing to see you that seizes me all of a sudden like cramps of tenderness; then the travel, the distraction of the present moment, makes it subside. But it is at night before I fall sleep that I spend thinking of you; and every morning when I awake you are the first thing that comes to my mind. [...] I still see you leaning on your elbow, your chin in your hand, dreaming with your sweet melancholy air. Remember, poor mother [...] that you will see me again next February. There's just the summer and the winter to go. [...]

December 15, 1850

Poor Old Darling,

When is there to be a wedding, you ask me, apropos of the marriage of Ernest Chevalier? When? Never, I hope. To the extent that a man is able to speak as to what he will do in the future, I respond here in the negative. The contact I have had with those with whom I've rubbed elbows a lot for the last fourteen months has made me retreat more and more into my shell.

Father Parain, who maintains that voyages change people, is mistaken when it comes to me. This is how I left and this is how I shall return, only with a bit less hair on my head and many more landscapes within it, that's all. As for my moral dispositions, I am keeping the same ones until further notice. And then, if I had to speak my deepest thoughts on the matter and if it were not too presumptuous, I would say: "I am too old to change. That ship has sailed."

When, as I have, one has lived an internally focused life full of turbulent analyses and contained flights of fancy, when one has so excited and calmed oneself successively and spent all of his youth maneuvering his soul as a rider does his horse [...] well then, what I mean to say is that if one has not already broken his neck at the beginning there is a good chance that he will not break it later.

I too am settled, in the sense that I have found my bearings, my center of gravity. I assume that no internal shake-up could ever displace me and make me fall to the ground. To me, marriage would be a horrifying betrayal. [...] The artist, I believe, is a monstrosity—something that defies nature. All of the suffering with which providence afflicts him comes from his stubborn determination to deny this axiom. He suffers for it and he makes others suffer for it. Just ask women who have loved poets and men who have loved actresses. Therefore this is my conclusion: I am resigned to live as I have lived—alone, with my group of great men who have been my circle, with my bear's skin, as I am bear-like myself. I couldn't care less about society, the future, what people might say, any kind of establishment, or even literary glory which used to make me spend so many white nights laying awake dreaming of it. This is how I am. This is my character.

The devil only knows where this two-page screed came from, poor dear lady. No, no—when I think of your gentle demeanor, so sad and so loving, of the pleasure I have living with you who are so full of serenity and earnest charm, I feel certain that I will never love another as I love you. [...]

Translated by Julie Grenet PhD, LP, from: Société des Eudes Littéraires Française (1974). *Correspondance 1850–1859—Oeuvres Complètes de Gustave Flaubert (Volume 13)*. Paris: Club de l'Honnête Homme.

MARCEL PROUST

Proust (1871–1922) published his masterpiece *In Search of Lost Time* in seven volumes, and it is considered one of the greatest novels of the twentieth century. Proust broke with convention and changed the shape of the novel as we know it from a linear narration and plot to an intimate subjective world.

His parents had great hopes for their son, but because of his poor health and the great amount of time he spent frequenting fashionable society, they worried he would be a failure. From age thirty-eight he spent the rest of his life writing his masterpiece. At the time of his death, he was not finished.

This letter to his mother was written less than a month after his father's death. He wrote it in the early hours of the morning while his mother was asleep in another room.

Proust had an extremely close relationship with his mother and he felt great pressure not to disappoint her. He was unable to tell her he was homosexual. He clung to her, yet resented her intrusion into his life. She chided him for being nocturnal and wanted him on a normal schedule. But he did his best work at night. He was forever a baby; she called him "my little wolf."

In a famous scene from his book, his grandmother offers him madeleines, which he dips into an infusion of tea. The sense memory of the taste and smells of the madeleines opens up strong memories of his past. He could not grow up and write his masterpiece with all its honesty and sexuality, all the complex feelings and lack of innocence, until his mother was gone.

December, 1903 (Age 32)

My dear little Mama,

I am writing you this little note while I'm finding it impossible to sleep, to tell you that I'm thinking of you. How I would love, and how ardently I wish, to soon be able to get up at the same time as you, to have my coffee and milk by your side. To feel that the hours we sleep and the hours we are awake are distributed over the same span of time would be, will be so charming to me. I had gone to bed at 1:30 with this aim but, after having had to get up again to take care of my needs, it was impossible for me to find my safety pin (which closes and tightens my bottoms). Suffice it to say that my night was kaput. I tried to find another one in your bathroom, etc. etc., and succeeded at nothing but catching a bad cold during this ambling (bad is in jest) but safety pins: none.

I went back to bed, but it was impossible to get any rest. All's well all the same; I am having a charming night making plans to live as you like and to live even more materially close to you, by living at the same times, in the same rooms, at the same temperature, according to the same principles, with mutual approval, if satisfaction is, alas, now to be denied us.* Forgive me for having left the desk of the smoking room in disorder, I was working so much up until the last minute. And as for this fancy envelope, it's the only one I have handy. Have Marie Antoine be quiet and leave the kitchen door, which carries her voice, closed.

A thousand tender kisses,
Marcel

I feel I'm going to sleep very well now.

Translated by Julie Grenet PhD, LP, from: Kolb, Philip (Ed.) (1953). *Marcel Proust: Correspondance avec sa Mère 1887–1905*. Paris: Librarie Plon.

Julie Grenet, PhD, LP, received her doctoral degree in French literature from Princeton University. She worked with psychoanalytic literary criticism before deciding to train at the National Institute for the Psychotherapies to become a licensed psychoanalyst. She has a full-time psychotherapy practice in New York City and enjoys working with speakers of both English and French.

---

*This remark about denied satisfaction is in reference to the recent death of Proust's father.

CHAPTER SEVEN

Poetry by people in analysis

The outpouring in response to my call for "Poetry by People in Analysis" was overwhelming. For some contributors, the writing added new levels of understanding to their therapeutic relationship. I asked our readers to suspend the expectation of scholarly tone and method usually found in psychoanalytic journals. For what we have here is not necessarily scholarly or polite.

Therapist and patient are collaborators in telling a story; some have been told a hundred times, and yet have never been told. Analysis is mutual storytelling. Some are simple stories told with staggering originality; some stories have the ability to glimpse change. What complicates the process is that each of us has multiple ways of telling our story. Have you wondered what story you are in at any given moment? An adventure story? A ghost story that haunts? A romantic one? A separation tale of standing up to a parent is a universal drama. One thing for sure, when you change the story, you change the storyteller.

Why do we write? For self-awareness, to tap into the unconscious, to access different self-states, to know who we are, for pleasure, for beauty, for clarity, to write ourselves into existence? We are searching for gold and scoop up the shimmering sand.

Several hundred thousand years after man learned to control fire, we got the idea of taking language and writing it down. The Minoans from ancient Crete invented the art of writing around 1650 BCE, a time known as the "creative prelude." One can see the two-sided clay disc called *Phaistos*, the most debated ancient written text in the world—consisting of 242 signs and symbols with an ideogrammatic script of unknown content, arranged in a spiral. The code has never been broken, and the content remains a mystery.

We are wired to write. I have found that writing can be a creative therapeutic tool with patients. Writing helps formulate chaotic fragments into a story. And it is in the telling of our story that we become who we are. Some patients come into treatment without a story, and part of our work as analysts is finding a cohesive narrative. Writing can take the split-off parts of ourselves, the dissociated parts, and bring those disowned parts into awareness. Once upon a time, in the beginning, there were caveman stories, bushman stories, Buddha and Christ stories. As Emily Dickinson, whose originality defies categorizing, said, "When it comes, the landscape listens, the shadow holds its breath." Ironically, to express an experience beyond words, the writer feels compelled to put that experience *into* words. And as analysts, when we talk about our patients, we can be poets.

Here are poems by people in analysis. Included in this section is a poem by psychoanalyst Robert Stolorow. One poet used a *nom de plume*. One poem is from a nine-year-old boy. Another poem, rather than capturing the carefree innocence of childhood, portrays instead childhood memories that are a time of dark hours, scary shadows, and harrowing obstacles. A few people wrote about their analysts; a few analysts submitted poetry, too. All grapple with understanding difficult and complicated feelings about loss and letting go, about growing up and growing old.

* * *

GRIEF CHRONICLES
ROBERT D. STOLOROW, PhD, PhD

These Grief Chronicles, written over an eight-year period, memorialize Dr. Daphne (Dede) Socarides Stolorow, who died at the age of thirty-four on February 23, 1991, four weeks after her cancer had been diagnosed.

1
Today I gave her ashes
to the sea she loved so much,
my loss its gain forever.
Goodbye my love.
The tide swooped in
and washed her from the death-black rocks
as I sat watching
with the stillness of a fallen gull
adding a few salty tears
to her new home.
Goodbye my love.

2
Today I visited her
as I do from time to time.
"Is it okay to feel happy again?"
I asked with nervous apprehension.
"Oh yes," she said,
holding my little-boy face
softly between her hands,
"I want that more than anything."
The warm glow of her smile
melted back slowly
into the sun-drenched sea.
Goodbye my love.

3
Each anniversary
(this the fifth)
I visit the sea
where I scattered her,
aging atheist,
conversing with an angel,

her smile,
knife-wound in my heart,
still warming.

4

It was a little scary
when I visited her last night,
shimmering midnight moon
lighting up the black, rocky home
where nine years she lay scattered,
pummeled by crashing, high-tide waves.
On the walk back to my car
after our yearly conversation
I figured out my life:
In its remains
I would give to others
the gift Dede gave to me.
Through me
her loving smile
will warm and brighten
those I love,
lifting us both
from the dark world of death
into the glow of life.

5

I wore the jacket
she picked for me
for 18 years
till it was torn and tattered,
leather showing holes,
frayed lining falling,
and I looked the homeless one
her dying left me.
When it was time
I left it
on a park bench by the sea
for my successor,
another homeless warmed
by Dede's gift to me.

Robert D. Stolorow, PhD, PhD, is a founding faculty member and training and supervising analyst at the Institute of Contemporary Psychoanalysis, Los Angeles, and a clinical professor of psychiatry at the UCLA School of Medicine. He is the author of more than fifteen books and 200 articles. He received his PhD in clinical psychology from Harvard in 1970, and a PhD in philosophy from the University of California in 2007. He received the Hans W. Loewald Memorial Award in 2012.

A SHORT POEM BY A NINE YEAR OLD
TERMINATING THERAPY
ANONYMOUS

Therapy is good
Therapy is bad
Therapy is the best thing
I ever had

ROSY GUILDENSTERN
OCTAVIO R. GONZALEZ, PhD

She stood five feet four,
red-brown hair, glasses.

Oblong shape, her nails
blunt, simple. Her nose

would wrinkle
as she urged me to keep talking

through snotty tissue.

Once I had to wait
in the narrow lobby

where a brown-haired
woman, faceless,

standing, blotted
soundless tears.

The amazing vitality

How ever did you
sponge so much

from so many of us
pulling our heads

from the sands
of our own stories.

There you sat, hands on lap

in a dark suit, pearls,
never yawning.

Octavio R. González, PhD, is assistant professor of English at Wellesley College, Massachusetts. His first poetry collection, *The Book of Ours* (Momotombo Press, 2009), was sponsored by Letras Latinas/The Institute for Hispanic Letters at the University of Notre Dame. His poetry also appears in *Puerto del Sol*, *MiPoesias*, and *OCHO*, among other journals. Octavio's research centers on transatlantic modernism, the twentieth-century novel, and intersectional queer studies. He is at work on a second poetry collection and his first monograph, tentatively titled *Misfit Modernism.*

* * *

THERAPY
SUSAN JASKO

I hate it when you move the furniture
and forget to change the calendar.
For three months it was November in Hawaii.

I pay you to look startled at my life.

Susan Jasko, MSW, is a graduate of the Child and Adolescent Psychoanalytic Psychotherapy Program at the National Institute for the Psychotherapies. She lives in St. Paul, Minnesota, and works as a psychotherapist with international survivors of politically motivated torture at the Center for Victims of Torture.

JACOB'S LADDER
ALISON BEYNON

Writing (mostly poetry and musings in a journal), has been an integral part of my eight-year therapeutic process with the Jungian analyst Elizabeth Martiny in Johannesburg, South Africa. Usually, the analytic experience has prompted me to write in order to take the exploration further, or to contain difficult feelings, or in some cases I have used Jung's idea of the active imagination to develop intimations I have had. I believe that writing has a huge potential for healing.

This is a poem written while working with unresolved grief at the death of my father when I was thirteen years old.

After the funeral
You came back in strange ways
Untimely comets across the night
Urgent Morse messages from crickets on the hill
An eternal sky-borne dressing gown
Sometimes in sleep
I felt your hand on my head
And your breathing my name back into me
Deep and slow

After the funeral
I commandeered you back in strange ways
Ravenous for the things that had defined you
The sharp-edged objects of everyday
That had etched you into me

I fingered your worn wallet, opening, closing,
I squirreled away your pen
Like a blind child learning Braille
I trailed my fingers across your books,
The Ex Libris with *your* name

I clung to the shape and smell of you
Once, cocooned in your wardrobe
I drowned in an ecstasy
Among your hollow suits

Even as your face greyed over
And slipped away from me
Your voice stayed
Emerging mostly at dusk
To call me on like a piper
From footprints ahead in the silver-wet sand
Where we had walked
From the anonymous crowd off the evening train
From the yellow glow of our windows
On the darkening hill

Year by year
Your shape broke up into
A thousand faint papery reflections
That hovered on fine subtle strings
Across my sky-line
Of home, hill and bay

But your words, still speaking to me,
Plaited themselves
Into a durable rope
The Jacob's Ladder
On which I climbed
Out of the bleakest years of my growing

Alison Beynon is a South African teacher and materials developer who has been running a literacy uplift project for disadvantaged and under-achieving students in the township of Alexandra in Johannesburg. She loves the freedom of writing poetry after the constraints and demands of educational writing, and feels hugely privileged to have enjoyed a long period in Jung-based therapy. She divides her time between Johannesburg, where her project is situated, and a village by the sea on the Cape coast, where she has embarked on writing a novel.

YOU

STEVE TURTELL

For Mr. M.

You would disapprove of this. And I'll hear
your disapproval next week, at our usual time.

"It's best to keep what goes on here private."
I asked you why and you didn't have an answer.

I don't know your first name but once did a reverse
search with your phone number. I have trouble

with boundaries, as you know. When you call
to reschedule I hear your lovely baritone:

"Mr. Turtell, this is Mr. M." Such old world formality;
the only instance of it in my life. You know more

about me than most, even my lover.
One measure of failure: everything I've

never told you. According to my one rule of therapy
everything I think to hold back is what I should say.

So that's why you know I want to fuck with you,
No, tell the truth, I want you to fuck me. That's why

I comment when your hair is longer and ask
"Becoming a hippy?" as I walk into the room,

you as always standing to the side, arms at your sides,
hands folded over one another just in front of your crotch

—protecting yourself? If I asked you'd say "Why do you
want to know that?", the usual game. For six years now

we've been playing together. I notice your middle
is nicely thickened and I try to sense the shape of your body

behind the Oxford button-down shirt, examine the serpentine
curve of your tie for clues to your chest, hope that one of these
days

I'll see signs of a meaty nipple pressing against the thick cotton.
I have great transference. You have a lovely smile. I've had
straight

therapists before. My first two while still a teenager
but I never had the hots for them and our therapy didn't last.

Steve Turtell is the author of *Heroes and Householders*. In 2010, his chapbook, *Letter to Frank O'Hara* won the Rebound Chapbook Prize given by Seven Kitchens Press. He is at work on a memoir, *Fifty Jobs in Fifty Years*, and *Peter Hujar: Invisible Master*.

PLAYGROUND OF DREAMS
ROSANNE TAYLOR

dear g-d
i need to play before i grow up,
so please—
   build me a playground
gated and safe
     a haven of freedom
where it's okay to let go
  of monkey bars
and drop
        d
        o
        w
        n.
dear g-d,
     cushion my falls
     don't let me be
          alone
on the slide
   and—dear g-d
   remember,
don't build it too high,
     slant it too steep
  or set too many steps;
   solder on rails
      to grasp
  when courage fails,
   soul and mind flail,
        when
white knuckled fingers
        of fear
   crawl up my spine
     eyeing the fall
       knowing

                                    i must
                                    plunge
                                        down
                                        the slope,

    inevitable as is breathing
and
dear g-d,
        soften
the floor
            beneath the slide,
    so i won't hurt
so bad
    when i fall.

dear g-d,
as you build
    my playground of dreams,
build
    at my level,
            my height
and some above
        for growing
and some lower
        for slowing
but no seesaws
        please.
i think
    i'd like to be done with those. dear g-d
        don't forget—
i'll need someone
            to stay
    and play
with me,
        remember
to give them
        the keys to my gate.

Rosanne Taylor lives in lower Manhattan with her husband and five children. Prior to having children she was a teacher and then a financial officer in a commercial company. Currently she is busy balancing her different roles as wife, mother, caregiver, and writer.

LEAVING THERAPY
ARTHUR TOBIAS

For Joan

All of a sudden it's time
the work we had to do together is done
as the realization hits
fear and confusion rise then settle
clear memories of the struggle
this intimate emotional relationship
how much your keen insight has meant to me
especially now in these last few sessions
tears rise but do not break
your eyes look wet to me
one good hug and out the door
no more questions except this
how do we learn to say goodbye

Arthur Tobias worked in the merchant marine and the Poets in the Schools Program and spent ten years as a graduate student in classical Chinese poetry. He is now a New York State licensed massage therapist, a certified Zero Balancer, and a teacher of the Alexander Technique. He lives with his wife in an intermittently empty nest in Manhattan. He wrote this poem forty years ago.

CHAPTER EIGHT

Voices out of New Orleans: Hurricane Katrina

Iow does the creative unconscious process trauma and catastrophic loss? For some, writing about the trauma helps work through what they had been unable to handle.

In 2005, the world watched with disbelief and horror as Hurricane Katrina, one of the five deadliest hurricanes in the history of the United States, thrashed furiously across New Orleans—leaving in its wake over 1,245 people dead and countless homeless. Like many, overwhelmed by scenes of the devastation, I felt a sense of profound helplessness.

On a hunch, I placed a call to Peter Cooley, a poet whose work I knew. Peter is a professor of English at Tulane University in New Orleans, and a member of a local poetry group. I asked him if he had any poems on Hurricane Katrina. "Are you kidding?" he said. "We have so many. We want our voices heard. We do not want to be forgotten." The meeting place for poetry readings had been destroyed by the hurricane, so the group had been meeting as nomads at various places around the ravaged city. Professor Cooley asked his students and colleagues to send me their poetry about Katrina. Lives were lost. Personal histories were lost. The poets of New Orleans would very much like their poetry read. So here are some of their voices: Professor Cooley, his daughter, his son, and one of his students at Tulane University.

* * *

AN AMERICAN SONNET (WRITTEN BEFORE KATRINA)
PETER COOLEY, PhD

This is my morning, mine. It will not come again.
Waking to our time together, reader, I have prayed
to the blue dark I stand up in, aching,
that we meet in my small words. But I am but wounded, too,
because I am a body, silly like you,
and ran too fast on the levee with the Mississippi
below me, the river accustomed to witness human suffering.
I have twisted my left foot. Hobbling, I cross the kitchen,
pour this coffee. How would you like yours?
Sugar? Butter on your toast? I have grape jelly
left over from my father's last day on earth.
Let's break bread together here on this line.

Peter Cooley, PhD, poet laureate of Louisiana, is professor of English, director of creative writing, and Senior Mellon Professor in the Humanities at Tulane University. He is the author of nine books, including *Night Bus to the Afterlife*, which deals with Hurricane Katrina.

EVACUATION
NICOLE COOLEY

The vanishing is supposed to unfold steadily but instead it happens all at once—

1.
My mother says: We are not leaving. This is our home.

The morning of the hurricane, far from New Orleans, my daughter sits at the kitchen table with crayons: I'm drawing weather.

The morning of the hurricane, the sky in New York is a glare of bright, bright blue. The 9/11 sky.

The morning of the hurricane in our last phone call, when I have given up yelling, begging, pleading with my parents to go, I tell my mother: Take the photo albums and leave them on a high shelf in the safest closet. One for me, Alissa and Josh, of our childhoods. To my father I ask: Do you have your poems?

2.
Supply List for my Brother on the Day of Reentry

A backpack if you have to walk to find them
Gas—full tank and safe closed containers to fill up
Water Jugs—assume you will be in N.O. for longer
Flashlights, matches
Flare spray and spare tire
A good map of the city for back routes
You can't take I-10!
Do you have a house key?

3.
First try to imagine what will be lost but keep it romantic: Live oaks in City Park. Japanese plum along St. Charles. The Victorian Mansion on the streetcar line where you were married.

The oyster shells in the parking lot in the West End, how you kicked up crushed white dust with your sister. The rope swing at the edge of the river on the levee where you hid with a high school boyfriend.

Or try to think rationally. There are agencies: FEMA. Red Cross. The
Louisiana State Police. There are hotlines.

All the phones are down. No landlines. No cell phones. No way, of
course, to reach them. Log on for news—
cnn.com (stream the video): "Watch the unanswered screams! Watch
the rooftop rescues!"
Then try to imagine them safe together: a house sealed shut, a water-
tight world of two.

I want the world to hush and stop and pay attention.

Nicole Cooley has published five books, most recently *Breach* (LSU
Press) and *Milk Dress* (Alice James Books), both in 2010. Her work has
appeared most recently in *The Rumpus*, *Drunken Boat*, and *Tinderbox*.
She is the director of the MFA Program in Creative Writing and Literary
Translation at Queens College, CUNY.

ELEGY FOR THE HURRICANE VICTIM
JOSH COOLEY

Here they are safe, no ocean.
No choppy churned-up house flogging
gulf. No pock-marked, skeletal
levees breached, no home's
eroded copingstones.
No bones.

No,
they are the rescued ones, they embraced
the helicopter crewmen, soared
into the sky. They rest in the
powdery underbelly of Houston's
city lights. They have spilled into
the Inner Loop, clogged up the Astrodome,
flooded the roads. And yet they are here,
my mother not among them.

No, she said again, again, to friends
I sent to rescue her. I know my son
will save me soon. No, really that's okay. No.

I am three weeks late, yes,
but heading home at dusk, I find myself
easing onto the highway, unpacked
and rushing back east and skipping the
exit signs. I want to come back
and find her still praying, the door
standing open, her outstretched arms, a broken
gutter collecting rainwater, drop by drop.

Josh Cooley, born and raised in New Orleans, is a graduate of Rice
University and Stanford Law School. He received an MA from Stanford
as well, and is now practicing law in California.

AFTER THE DESTRUCTION
LAUREN RUTH

This poem began as an assignment for Professor Peter Cooley's creative writing class.

I cannot look into his eyes
without seeing the burned out lights

and glossy, oil-stained surfaces
of St. Bernard, his childhood home.

He cannot close his eyes without
seeing the faces of the dead

and hearing voices of old friends
now lost beneath a tarnished crust.

I smelled stale mold encase his clothes
and waded through the knee-deep sludge

but these remains did not seem real
till consecrated with his tears.

He choked on soft sobs when he found
his shredded teddy bear in mud

then wept a hurricane for time
now piled in a heap of junk.

Although I held his clammy hands
and viewed the carnage by his side,

I cannot understand his pain.
I cannot give him back his life.

Through soggy lips and hallowed cheeks
his eyes are dead like St. Bernard.

Lauren Ruth works as an advocate for nonprofits at the Connecticut state legislature and is finishing her PhD in social psychology at Yale University. She lives in New Haven with her two Hurricane Katrina rescue mutts.

CHAPTER NINE

Presence and absence

Presence and absence. Connection and separation. What are the ways we hold on to another even when that person is not physically present? Exploring these questions is part of what happens in psychotherapy. It also happens in writing. Stories carry both memory and longing and offer moments so vivid that both writer and reader become immersed in their sensual vitality. In memory, no one is ever absent; rather, persons we've lost continue to inhabit an emotional inner landscape, infused with the treasure of what they mean to us.

In writing about his psychiatrist father, Mark Singer, also a psychiatrist, draws an inner portrait of a man who strongly influenced him. "When my dad retired, I inherited some of his patients. Writing about him was a bittersweet experience that evoked the notion of memory and the passage of time. My father took great interest in the stories of people's lives. He seemed to be particularly moved by nostalgic experience. He seemed to find comfort in the ways that a feeling of loss could be paradoxically linked to a feeling of pleasure. And how a sense of longing for the past could be affectionately fastened to a quality of hope for the future." Mark Singer wrote this story in the months before his father died.

Rachael Matthews is a poet from England who grew up in a small seaside town where her ancestors were circus performers. The two poems included here are taken from her sequence, *Family Circus*, which formed part of her doctoral dissertation. She paints portraits with words, as she writes about relationship, risk, the body, entrances and exits: the stuff of every real (and imagined) performance in the "sawdust circle."

David Austern contributes two poems about the death of his father, who drowned when David was an adolescent—and the effect it has had on him throughout his life. These poems explore the impact of trauma, offering radically different illustrations of attempts at coping. The poems beg the question of whether writing itself can serve as a therapeutic tool in the face of terrible loss.

Judith Lit, the author of "Absence," is an American documentary filmmaker who lives in France five months of the year. In this piece, she writes of her connection with a neighbor, an elderly farmer who lived a life very different from her own. Despite their lack of similarities, a bond grew between them in surprising ways; a relationship took root in their mutual love of the land and nature. How do we hold on to someone long after they are gone? The author discovers that her connection to the earth is so primal that she is irrevocably linked to her now-absent friend.

Presence is a quality of being. We may recognize it in great works of music and art, in moments of oneness with nature, in the moving novel, story, and poem—and sometimes even in our better analytic hours. Yet, absence and presence will always remain in dialectical tension because they each contain the essence of the other.

* * *

UNBROKEN CHAIN
MARK SINGER, MD

After over fifty years of treating patients, my father, a psychiatrist, took down his shingle. He picked a day to stop practicing, saw his last few patients, stepped out of his office, closed the door, and walked away. In the end, after thousands of forty-five minute sessions of talking, listening, and helping, ironically, he said only, "It's time to stop." He was leaving behind a lifetime.

He was not turning back, but neither was he turning his back. Not on a half century of patients and their stories. Stories of sadness and of joy. Of wishes and fears. Misery and hope. Suffering and triumph. Bitter stories and sweet ones. Stories of despair and of fulfillment. Of accommodation and rebellion. Freedom and constraint. War stories and stories about making peace. Angry stories, guilty stories, lonely stories, and love stories. But mostly, stories about all the conflict and beauty in between. The stories of our lives.

How does one walk away from the relationships with patients? Patients with whom one has spent years together at sea. Straining, struggling, and delighting in intangible moments of connection that seem to hold much of the meaningfulness? How does one walk away from being immersed, day after day, year after year, in the winding and jagged paths, the various and sorted twists and turns of lives lived. And all of the sorrow, satisfaction, envy, frustration, pride, shame, angst, gratification, regret, and pleasure that comes with. Most of all, how does one walk away from the sheer privilege of sitting down with another human being, and together, trying to untangle it all.

We never know in this work, when a patient walks through the door for the first time, if this will be the one and only session we will have together, or if it will mark the beginning of a relationship that will span a good chunk of a century. Will they be here and gone in a relative instant, or will this person sitting with me today, a stranger, be a person I will come to know in some ways better than my own children and together with whom I will grow old.

One of the patients my father said goodbye to recently had been a patient of his continuously since 1965. When this patient walked in the door of my father's office for the first time, Lyndon Johnson was president. US troops were not yet on the ground in Vietnam. The patient, at the time, was in his twenties. He is now in his seventies, a grandfather.

How does the patient walk away from my father? A patient with such bad anxiety that it flirts with psychosis. He is often frightened and is delusional at times. For forty-seven years he has sought relief in my father. He trusted him. He was calmed by him. The patient told my father that what he did for him was "magic." Sometimes it helps to have magical thinking.

How does one even give up a decades-old office phone number? A phone number that has traveled with my father to all of his many offices over the years. A number that I have known since I was a child. In the era before email, websites, and texting, it was through that one phone number that a career's worth of patients reached my father. Originally on rotary phones, dialing it up in times of need, times of crisis, times of everything. It was through that number that my father put food on the table and as patients like to say, "sent his kids to college." And it was through that number that all of the relationships, over all the years, began. The phone number was, in many ways, a lifeline.

So how does it all come to an end? How did the shingle, dripping with history and still pulsing with life, get put away? Not so easily. Not so fast.

As for the phone number? My father had the line installed in his home. He told me, "You never know when someone might want to call." It struck me that he was not installing the phone number at his home, but where he lived. He was staying connected. To who he was. To others. To being alive.

As for the patient, what will happen to him? Just as my father was reluctant to leave his patient, the patient, as one might imagine, was reluctant to leave him. As it turns out, my father transferred the care of his patient to me, and he would now become my patient. Just before the termination of their relationship, after all the years, my father offered some final parting words of comfort to the patient he had known the longest, and with whom he had spent a lifetime. He said, with a knowing smile, "Don't worry, my son has the magic too." The words were comforting. To all three of us.

Just a few months after closing his practice, my father passed away.

The next generation of talking and listening will carry on. Going forward, there will be more winding and jagged paths, more twists and turns, and more stories to tell, all told, as we move further, along an unbroken chain.

We live within each other. Within each other we live on.

Mark Singer, MD, is a psychiatrist in private practice in New York City. He is on the faculty of New York Medical College and at the Manhattan Institute for Psychoanalysis, and is a candidate at the New York University Postdoctoral Program in Psychotherapy and Psychoanalysis.

BIRTHDAY PARTY
RACHAEL MATTHEWS, PhD

I bring a card with stitched-on, tactile dinosaur
saying three today in twenty point comic sans.
Before torn paper and red cake
my brother shows me around like an estate agent
talking in a written-down way: *due to* instead of *because*,
all euphemism and platitude.
It's a language on loan and he seems glad to have it
after months on mute. I do what he wants:
praise the sterile new rooms of his house,
remembering how he sledgehammered them dead
on broken news of our mother's *exit strategy*,
what he calls *that stunt with a knife*.
His taut wife beckons me, fiddling with bunting.
You have to do something—
he keeps cleaning things, won't let me breathe,
goes to bed with a headache thinking it's the end.
Through a doorway I watch him with his son—
blue-eyed, blond, the same-shaped head.

THE RIDE
RACHAEL MATTHEWS, PhD

Driving back from the rollercoaster
we're lulled by our level progress;
talked out from reliving the second dip
much bigger than the first, and more sudden.

This time our mother tipped and slid
within a week; began rattling inside
the carriage of her own bones.

So we send gifts and visit.
My brother brings his kids,
holds up the new baby as if to the light.

While she sleeps we escape,
try to laugh at the fairground but fail
until we find hilarity in sudden freefall.

There's a queue of cars
heading off the promenade.

You're quiet, what are you thinking about?
whispers my brother over his shoulder—
checking whether five year olds
get lost in dark tunnels too.

Godzilla, says a voice
slack with distraction.

We draw up outside her house;
at first nobody moves to get out.

Rachael Matthews, PhD, grew up in England and now lives in New York where she's a psychoanalytic candidate. Her research at Sussex University explored creativity and mental health. Her poems have appeared in UK anthologies and literary magazines. She paints, plays the piano, and travels to very remote islands. A former BBC radio news broadcaster, she still enjoys making the weather forecast rhyme.

EXCORIATION
DAVID AUSTERN, PsyD

I remember the razor my uncle gave me
for 8th grade graduation—Remington Electric,
water-resistant. A favor, maybe. My father

dead but rising from the space between
my lips and nose. Stubble then. Still,
I'd scratch at him with charged metallic

as if he'd disappear. All I did was push
him deeper. Now he's so ingrown
I tweeze him out. Post-shower,

after the mirror defogs, I press up against it
and inspect. My skin's thin enough
to see him lurking underneath, curling back

into my cheeks. Sometimes I think he's buried
there, hiding in each bump, each pustule.
I'll bleed to free him. To be free of him?

After he drowned there was no one
to teach me how to shave, how to go
with the grain—face down, neck up.

Sometimes I wonder if I'll keep doing
all the wrong things, if it's just his way
of saying *I won't leave you again.*

DÉNOUEMENT
DAVID AUSTERN, PsyD

If I'm my own protagonist then most of my goodbyes
have been disappearances. The father character
drowned; ex-girlfriends skipped town,

sent postcards. The problem now is I need
a real ending. I'm supposed to terminate
a year's worth of work, to write myself

out of this chapter. I flip back a thousand pages
to when I was afraid of the phone.
It only brought bad news

and when I'd dial nobody picked up. The toughest call
I made was the one for help, the aha moment
there was conflict in my narrative.

But this story is sci-fi and nothing dies of natural causes.
When my first therapist graduated, finished
school, started a practice,

the couch cushions exploded with foam. Her eyes
were black holes, thematic echoes of other
abruptions—an uncle dropping dead

in an airport, an aunt embolizing. If this were *Lost*,
the monster would swallow these people
in smoke, pluck them from ink

to white space. If this were a song, I'd pray for the music
to slowly fade, for the only aural trace to be
nothing like a whimper or a bang.

David Austern, PsyD, MFA, is a clinical psychology with a specialty in
anxiety and related disorders. He earned his doctorate at Rutgers University, his master's in poetry at the University of Michigan, and he has
a particular interest in writing-based PTSD treatments.

ABSENCE
JUDITH LIT

For the ninth year now, the terrace is covered with walnuts. What with the muddy trenches and mayhem from the irrigation work in course, I haven't attempted to haul out the drying trays. Instead, I've emptied baskets of nuts directly onto the stone floor as Monsieur Gonzales used to do before I had trays made. I roll them about with a broom so they'll dry evenly, with the same familiar clatter and motion as his. In fact, because the nuts are now only one layer deep and the wind from the north sweeps with regularity across the terrace, the nuts are drying in record time. His method was the right one after all. How elegant and restrained he was about my naïve attempt to give professionalism to our little enterprise by having the local carpenter build us drying trays. Never a word of criticism, just a shake of the head and a shift to doing things my way. Will I ever stop missing him?

The wind in the plane tree and the dry scuttle of leaves across the gravel are suddenly broken by a wild calling from the direction of La Tache. I run through the gate just as a dark wedge of cranes (*les grues*) knifes through the sky headed toward warmer lands. When the wild cranes pass, the cold isn't far behind.

Today is La Toussaint (All Saints' Day). The first Toussaint since he died. Yesterday, I took flowers to his grave. From the small, windswept cemetery, I could make out the ridge top to the north, where his farm and mine hug the swell of high meadow. This morning, with his family and all the village arriving for Mass and the priest's blessing of the tombs, I couldn't bring myself to go, preferring instead a day of solitude, tying up bushes that could break in winter wind, re-staking young fruit trees, restacking wood in the garage.

I work with a slow persistence, stopping occasionally to brush the hair from my face with the back of my forearm, a gesture foreign to my urban life, the same gesture that I've seen the neighbor woman down the road make when she looks up from her work in the field, taking a minute to recognize me before she waves. Now I repeat her gesture naturally, falling into the rhythm of earth and sky.

Monsieur Gonzales came attached to this land when I purchased it nine years ago. The isolation of our farms meant that he was my only close neighbor. The morning after I arrived, I found him in my meadow, a small, fine-boned man in a threadbare, once-stylish tweed jacket, tall rubber boots, and wool cap, leaning on his staff as he guarded his cows. And so, his presence on my farm was a fact that went unquestioned. He grazed his cows, tended the meadow, and helped with the walnut harvest. The irascible recluse of the region became my friend. Together, we cut fallen trees after a storm. We left offerings of mushrooms and chestnuts in front of one another's door. Sitting in front of the fire, he taught me about badgers and boar, and I answered his questions about city life and America. Our dialogue spanned not only continents but centuries. We also fought. Standing in the dirt road that runs along the ridge top, we screamed at each other when his freely wandering bull once again had damaged my fruit trees or when he had cut down a majestic oak for firewood, and he insisted that my gentle attentions and occasional treats for his dog had destroyed her motivation to herd his cows. Such an exchange might be followed by months of proud petulance, but sooner or later one of us would find an excuse for contact, and, the silence broken, our dialogue would resume.

"His death marks the end of an era," several people said to me at the funeral months ago. Holding fast to the old ways, Monsieur Gonzales lived on a broken-down farm without heating or plumbing, cooked on his wood fire, and shot off his gun to ward away intruders. With an outlaw mentality, he ran his cows through other people's fields under the cover of night when he had nothing left to feed them.

He died in the fullness of summer. "We're gathered here to bid adieu to one of our own," began the apple-cheeked priest presiding at the funeral in the solid little village church on an already oppressive July morning. "He may have been different, and he may have been rough around the edges and caused a few scandals, but he was a man of passion and his passion was the earth. He was in love with the land, with nature, and with his animals; and if they meant more to him than people, perhaps that's not a lesser love."

The cranes' sharp lament has given way to autumnal music smoothing their wake with rustling crescendos and golden light. I pause to stand in the meadow, breathing in a world that has become dear to me. This is where my neighbor is, not at the cemetery. He is here in the rippling of the forest edging the meadow, in the thud of falling chestnuts, in the sun igniting the stone wall, in the marauding of wild boar in the orchard, and the scampering of a lithe grey fox. He is here in the hooting of an owl in the night air. My neighbor wasn't a man living with nature but rather an aspect of nature itself, with his brusque retorts, his silent step, his fury and humor, his eloquent gesticulations and wry smile, his moments of surprising tenderness. Like the roe deer and the hawk, he was of this place. I think to myself how arrogant we human beings are to imagine ourselves separate from the landscape that bears us, nourishes us, forges our spirit with harsh realities, and then claims us at last.

The wood stacked neatly at the far end of the garage, I close the door. Night is falling with a rapidity that spells the approach of winter. Above the line of darkened trees on the ridge top to the west, a sliver of moon is now visible and a single, nearby star shines with cold intensity. This is the quiet time, before the night birds begin calling to each other. Down the dirt road, the door of Mr. Gonzales's farmhouse is locked, and pigeons fly in and out of broken upstairs windows. Despite the lines of memory that tie him to this land, in the shimmering silence there is a new emptiness.

Judith Lit, a documentary filmmaker for more than twenty-five years, has focused her work on environmental and social issues. Award-winning films include: *Dark Circle*, *Voices from the Classroom*, and most recently, *After Winter, Spring*, an intimate portrait of farmers in the Périgord region of southwest France. Judith divides her time between New York City and a small farm in the Périgord.

CHAPTER TEN

Emotional travel writing

One way of travelling is to throw away the Michelin Guide and read a good book set in the region you're visiting and let the book guide you to discover beauty in unexpected corners. In this way a traveler can go off on a different kind of journey, one where she searches for the visceral world of a historical person by retracing the emotional places in that person's life.

One summer not long ago, I visited friends from New York who had bought a house in Arezzo, Tuscany. In a letter they told me that Michelangelo's birthplace was only an hour's drive away. My imagination went wild. I had to make a pilgrimage to the birthplace of this Renaissance man, one of the greatest inventive and tormented geniuses ever born. Curious about his internal space and creative process, I was impelled to follow his footsteps. I hear Michelangelo's words, "Remember, the map is not the terrain."

Five hundred years after he created his masterpieces—the Sistine Chapel ceiling, the Pieta, and his David—I set off on an adventure in search of this man who reinvented art, with his life as the raw material. I started at the house where he was born, in the small village of Caprese. Then on to Florence and the Galleria dell'Accademia to see his David and the Bearded Slave, chiseled out of Carrera marble. Michelangelo glimpsed the slave in the marble and carved until he set him free. That same afternoon I went to his final resting place, the Santa Croce Basilica, where his tomb is cradled by marble sculptures. Nearby lay other geniuses—his eternal neighbors—Galileo, Rossetti, and the empty tomb of Dante.

A prolific poet, Michelangelo wrote over 300 sonnets and madrigals in which he lays bare his troubles, doubts about himself, his desires, and shame.

LOVE'S JUSTIFICATION
Michelangelo Buonarroti (1475–1564)

His hope is treacherous only whose love dies
With beauty, which is varying every hour;
But, in chaste hearts uninfluenced by the power
Of outward change, there blooms a deathless flower,
That breathes on earth the air of paradise.

Translated by William Wordsworth (1770–1850)

* * *

THE DAY OF MICHELANGELO
BONNIE ZINDEL, LCSW

It is my long-anticipated August break. I arrive in Arezzo from Rome on the fast train, and then take a taxi to a little restaurant in the center of town. The restaurant is filled for the evening hour.

There they are as planned, Margaret and Roberto, sitting at a corner table with friends and family—celebrating their daughter, Frederica's, sixteenth birthday. And as her godmother, I measure her emotional growth, like inches marked with pencil on the wall.

I met Margaret and Roberto on the gynecologist's waiting-room floor at 91st Street and Park Avenue in New York a week before Margaret and I both gave birth. My husband did not want to attend the classes, so Roberto coached us two expectant mothers on our birthing breaths. I felt I was giving birth as a single mother. Where was Tom?

In the restaurant in Arezzo, Margaret rushes over, smiling and radiant. "Hello, hello," she says. "You must not know what time you're on." She helps me off with my jacket.

"What time is it?" I ask.

Roberto greets me with a warm hug. "Nearly ten-thirty, Italian country time. You look wonderful," he says. "Try this. *Panza panzarotti*. The porcini mushrooms are from the village. You go to the market and ask what was just pulled from the earth and then you cook it."

"I'm too excited to be hungry. One thing I must do while I'm here is get to Michelangelo's house."

"Then you must go tomorrow, it's only open on Friday," he says.

Margaret shakes her head. "No honey, it's only open on Saturday morning."

The two always seemed well suited to each other, even though Roberto grew up in Italy and Margaret grew up in the Midwest.

Later, at their villa, built in the thirteenth century by a king who gave it to his daughter as a wedding present, I unpack on the stone floor, above the royal chambers where my friends now live. I close the shutters tight, pull out two books, *The Sonnets of Michelangelo* and *A Year of Reading Proust*, and place them next to a vase with freshly cut wildflowers.

"Goodnight," they call up the stairs.

I bundle up in two warm sweaters and a pair of white socks and climb into the canopy bed. This is the first time I am traveling without Tom. I didn't know that sleeping in castles could be so very chilly, and I bury myself in two additional blankets, wrapping them tightly around me like a cocoon.

The next morning, I borrow Margaret and Roberto's dark-green Fiat and pull out of the driveway past lavender and red geraniums in clay pots. I drive forty minutes through the Tuscan hills.

I feel good being alone with my thoughts for a few hours. I feel protective of these times. Maybe too much. The sun feels warm and restorative, and I wish I could stay here forever. One has to move on in one's life, take chances, do new things. And here on vacation seems a perfect time to expect the unexpected.

I drive along a winding road to the entrance of Michelangelo's birthplace. It is quiet, serene, and the only sound is the chattering of morning birds and the pebbles under my feet. No one is around. The air smells sweet and new, perfumed by pines and fir trees. I feel a little nervous, like a guest marching into a past millennium and viewing a holy sanctuary of brilliance.

Up the hill, along a dirt road, is the house where Michelangelo was born, a simple three-story stone farmhouse with steps leading to an archway. Across from the house is a smaller building of the same material. He carved in stone and lived in stone.

I look out at the panoramic view toward the Tuscan hills that Michelangelo saw 500 years ago, when as a child he gazed across the sprawling valley. Not far from this spot lie the Carrera quarries that nurtured this child of marble.

No one is around. Is this really the right house? I ring the bell but no one answers. I cross to the door of the smaller building and ring again. I hear rustling inside. A man in his sixties appears, pulling a blue cable-knit sweater over his head. He seems a bit ragged. I surmise that he's the gatekeeper and host to the occasional visitor.

"It is closed at this hour," the hermit-like caretaker says, whiskey on his breath. He coughs into his hand.

I move closer. "But I have come so far to see this. No one seemed to know the opening times."

He shrugs his shoulders.

"Can't you just let me in?"

The recluse shakes his head, a clump of gray hair falls over his forehead.

"Ohhh," I say, crestfallen. I'm surprised at how much this means to me.

The hermit straddles the doorway and responds to my disappointment, as if wanting to give me something for my trip. "He was born here in 1475. As a baby, he was sent to a wet nurse for a while, the wife of a stonecutter in Carrera, then was returned to his mother." The hermit seems to be speaking more to himself than to me. He scratches his cheek. "His mother died when he was six. She was twenty-six."

"So young, both of them." I am thankful he didn't close the door on me. Now he seems almost friendly, maybe even happy to see a face, any face. I'm surprised how well he speaks English. He leads me toward the main house.

"Here, maybe you can peek through the window," he offers, taking me up a few steps. "The kitchen."

I picture Michelangelo with his mother. While she kneads stone-ground flour and water, her young son takes dough from the chestnut table and, in his hands, sculpts tall bell towers and imaginary birds.

The hermit puts his hands in his pockets and shifts his weight. "His father was left with five sons. Michelangelo was the second born." The hermit holds up two fingers. "He and his father weren't close. The father had a hard time handling so many sons alone." He says this as if telling it for the first time. "At thirteen, Michelangelo left home to apprentice at the studio of Ghirlandaio. By fourteen, he was studying sculpture at a school in the Medici garden. And he *never* came back."

"Never? Why not?"

The hermit shrugs. "He never stopped working. Once, when he was seventeen, he was out of work. But only for a short time. He always wanted a connection to his father, always wanted his respect, and did not get it until his father's last days. When his father died, Michelangelo was overcome. Overcome with grief. Terrible for him. Oh, his father did not want him to be an artist!"

The hermit gestures around the grounds as an invitation. "Walk around."

I smile. I hadn't expected such an internal guide, and someone so articulate. "You sound like an art historian."

He says nothing, escorts me a bit further. "He was a melancholy boy. Sometimes quick-tempered, getting into fights. His nose was flattened twice. He was passionate and mercurial, a temperamental genius." His tone lightens. "But friends found him funny, kind, and generous. He was determined, but could not just summon up his inspiration at will. He was never beholden to anyone. He was no ordinary mortal."

We stop, looking out over the valley. "Beautiful, huh?" the hermit says.

"Very."

As he walks away, I look out at the hills and wonder. Did this young illuminist mix paints out of sand and coralberries and with a spatula from the kitchen squeeze the juice out to paint with his fingers? Or while wandering from view, did he find a piece of iron from discarded window railings and, with red poppies and twigs, create a masterly portrait of a tree only to have it be carried away by the next wind?

I walk to the other side of the property and stare out at the fir trees from this different perspective. Years ago, he cut some of these trees from his early days and sent them down the River Arno. The wood with the scent of his musky youth, log by log, formed a flotilla of timber, sailing to the Sistine Chapel, to cradle him as he painted.

I turn back and head to the smaller building, but when I knock on the door, there is no answer. I look around, but no sign of the hermit. I wonder if he's taking an afternoon nap. I open my purse and jot down a quick note of thanks before heading back to the car.

* * *

The lulling sound of a downpour filters through the third floor of the Hotel Loggiato dei Serviti in Florence. After a simple breakfast, I head to the flower market. I keep thinking about the hermit and his incredible sensitivity, how tuned-in he was to Michelangelo's inner life. Is he okay living like that? I wish I'd asked. He couldn't be just the caretaker. Did he drop out of some high-pressure job for a simpler life?

One advantage of traveling alone is speaking to interesting people. I would not have spoken to the hermit if I had been with someone else. Like my ex-husband, Tom. He liked to keep to himself.

Even though I had been divorced for well over a year, today, standing in front of the gardenias at the flower market, I suddenly realize that I am really alone. And that I am in Florence without him. Turning left, I head toward the Galleria dell'Accademia.

The rain has kept people away and I walk right into a huge room full of Michelangelo. Right in front of me is the Bearded Slave, *Schiavo Barbuto*. The slave emerges from a block of Carrera marble, formed millions of years ago when the earth was cooling and held together by centripetal forces. I remember reading that every piece of marble has a different grain, and each piece has its own human-like fingerprint.

This block of marble, Michelangelo said, contained the slave reawakening. The slave had been waiting to be released for eons—not with a chisel and hammer—but with his own fortitude and will. What is he thinking, this prisoner looking out? The affliction of slavery marks his face. His deep-set eyes seek vitality and spark.

I leave the museum. As I wander toward the Duomo and Michelangelo's Pieta, still under the spell of the tormented figure struggling for release, I suddenly realize that today would have been Tom's and my anniversary.

I weave through some side streets. The rain has stopped and I put my umbrella in my bag. I cross the street surprised to find myself in front of Dante's studio. It is closed for renovation.

There is a man selling gelato, and I buy a small cup of *Tartufido Chocolata*.

I'm at a loss, with no plans for the day. A view of a church dome appears in the distance. I start walking in that direction, as Michelangelo must have done hundreds of years ago; I follow in his footsteps.

The road opens onto a piazza, and I step into another century—the church with its Renaissance dome stands before me. I look up and realize I have fallen upon the Basilica di Santa Croce.

I walk inside and my eyes squint and adjust to the darkness, pierced by an occasional glistening of refined gold. A woman guide in a full blue cotton skirt and lighter blue sweater is speaking English to two American couples who listen attentively.

"Rossini is there," she points, "and his neighbor, Galileo, here. This is the graveyard of geniuses." The guide continues to walk. "In the two adjacent chapels are some of Giotto's frescoes." She turns her back slightly. "There to the right of the altar is the Giotto painting of St. Francis at his moment of death. Giotto's style was revolutionary and caused quite a stir. He shifted the emphasis from the glorification of God to the glory of human life, and with it, he ushered in the Renaissance." I stand there in awe.

The guide straightens her blouse as she leads them to Dante Alighieri. "This is a monument, not a tomb. Dante is buried in Ravenna, where he died." She pauses.

I remember in my junior year of high school when my English teacher, Miss Delafield, held Dante's *Inferno* tightly to her chest, peered over her metal-rimmed spectacles, and said to the class in a trembling voice, "*I mezzo cammin di nostra vita, mi ritrovai per una selva oscura che la diritta via era smarrita.*" "In the middle of the journey of life I find myself in a dark wood where the straight path is lost."

The guide gazes at the monument and quotes from Dante's *Paradiso*: "The love that moves the sun and the other stars." *"L'amor che muove ile sole e l'altre stelle."*

I keep my distance from the two couples. One of the husbands rolls up his plaid sleeves and frames a shot with his Minolta. His wife murmurs to him in a Southern accent, glancing at me. I feel like an intruder.

The guide moves to the tomb next to Dante. "I saved this for last," she says. The two couples huddle closer.

In the coolness of the sanctuary, the cadence of the guide's impassioned English, spoken with her Italian accent, is mesmerizing. "The golden candles are for the angels." I have no choice but to follow her. "I saved this for last," the guide repeats. "Here lies Michelangelo Buonarroti.

"He died in Rome when he was ninety years old, and his body was stolen by his nephew one hot July day and returned to Florence—rightfully so—where he belongs. This is where he wanted to be buried, right here in this spot where we stand. He picked this spot many years before his death so he could be within view of the Duomo when the doors open to Paradise. In his will he left his soul to God and his body to the earth."

I stare at his tomb, astonished that I have wandered here unintentionally.

The guide continues. "He loved walking the streets and squares, imagining. The tomb is sculpted in the style of Michelangelo and I think he would be pleased with it." My eyes glisten. The two American women listen attentively as their husbands shuffle on the periphery.

"Near the end, he said to a friend, 'I have reached the twenty-fourth hour of my day.' He was not afraid of death. He figured if God had created such a good life for him on earth, the same must be waiting for him in heaven." The guide pauses; she seems interested in my reaction.

"Architect and painter, but mostly he thought of himself as a sculptor, capturing the emotional tensions of humanity in Carrera marble. Michelangelo believed that marble, not yet carved, holds the form of every idea the greatest artist ever had."

I wonder if that is why he left the Slave unfinished.

"It was said that with his left hand he sculpted the brilliance of sunshine and its softer tones of yellow." The guide continues. "And with his right hand, he sculpted the feelings of night, darker colors, browns and grays. Dark absorbs time. For him, art was the most profound aspiration of the human spirit."

The guide moves closer to the sepulcher and stands there silently for a moment. I also move closer. One of the wives, the taller one, with a large jade necklace, takes notes in a spiral binder. I imagine she works as a freelance journalist for a newspaper back home.

After his David, the Pieta, the Slaves, the Sistine Chapel, the Last Supper, architectural domes, the politics of art, the fighting and the loving, the struggles of family, the glory of creation, and the inner hopes and torment, it all comes down to this. This dreamless place of nature that summons us, that inevitable moment, big or small, little or giant, it calls us, even Michelangelo. Here, a man, like any man, he lies.

The couples walk away and I stay behind alone. I close my eyes, and in the darkness I wonder. What were his final thoughts in the twenty-fourth hour? Did he see all his work pass before his eyes or witness his life flash in front of him? Did he see all the sculptures in marble that he had not yet released? I like to imagine him as a boy in Caprese, playing in the Tuscan hills, crushing coralberries into pigments as his mother sings to him. All of that—and here he is. A marble tomb.

I hear the guide wind down the tour. I turn around and listen.

"I invite you to visit the Duomo and make sure to see Michelangelo's final Pieta at the Museo del Bargello."

The two couples walk off, thanking the guide profusely. I'm happy to see them leave, and linger behind, waiting. The guide slips on her coat and folds a paisley scarf into a triangle around her neck, tying the ends in a knot.

I watch but do not want the woman to leave. I need something but don't know what. I walk up to her; she seems surprised by my approach.

"Excuse me, would you talk to me for a moment?" is all I can say.

The woman hesitates, glances at her watch, and then exhales. "All right. But just a moment."

Unable to find words, I stand there, surprised by the avalanche of unexplained feelings that overtake me. "I ... I ..." No words form. The guide stands patiently, her expression curious. Then without awareness, I burst into tears, tears from a place that catches me by surprise. I try to catch my breath. The guide stands there.

I shrug my shoulders in wonder. "I don't know why I'm crying." A part of me feels so foolish, and yet so right, standing there like a child.

The guide places her hand on my shoulder. "I understand." She looks at me knowingly.

Almost laughing through tears, I'm still unable to speak. Then, after a long while, I look into the guide's face. "It is being in the presence of the divine."

The guide nods. "Yes."

We stand together silently in a strangely comfortable place. Then, after a few moments, the guide smiles. "Arrivederci," she says, pulling her belt tighter around her beige coat and walking out of the basilica through large wooden doors into the early evening. I watch as the guide disappears from view.

Bonnie Zindel, LCSW, is a faculty member, and supervising and training analyst at the National Institute for the Psychotherapies in New York. She is a founding editor and creative literary editor of *Psychoanalytic Perspectives*. She is the author of "A Bird that Thunders: An Analysis with Emmanuel Ghent," in *Clinical Implications of the Psychoanalyst's Life Experience* (Routledge, 2013). Bonnie has conducted writing groups for psychotherapists for over twenty years. A playwright and novelist (HarperCollins, Viking, Bodley Head), Bonnie is a former member of the Actors Studio Playwrights Unit. She has most recently written a play, *My Simone*, based on the life of Simone de Beauvoir, which has been performed in New York.

CHAPTER ELEVEN

The unexpected poet: D. W. Winnicott

D. W. Winnicott was an English pediatrician and psychoanalyst best known for his ideas on the true self and the false self, and the transitional object. Central to Winnicott's work is his vision of creativity, which he saw as fundamental to being human. He believed that life without creativity is not worth living and is equivalent to psychic death. He is not talking here about the creativity of a genius like Cezanne or James Joyce, but the creativity accessible to all of us—an aliveness and originality in our everyday life. Winnicott encourages us to leap off the beaten path. At his 1970 lecture to the Progressive League in London, Winnicott said that to draw like Picasso one has to *be* Picasso. He was saying that we each need to be our own original self.

When one thinks of Winnicott, certain attributes come to mind: originality, spontaneity, playfulness, freedom, and paradox. He was interested in imaginative living. For him, it is in the transitional space between the inner and outer world that creativity occurs, an area of interest to philosophers and poets—who, Freud acknowledged, discovered the unconscious long before he did.

Winnicott loved poetry. He said that the poet in him "reaches to a whole truth in a flash" and carries with it enormous feelings. Winnicott found kindred spirits among the poets and artists of the Romantic period, especially Wordsworth and Keats. He felt an affinity for their appreciation of the authentic, spontaneous individual and the high value they placed on creativity and imagination. The Romantics privileged the inner life of feelings rather than formal rules imposed from outside (Goldman, 1993).

In both Wordsworth and Keats we can hear poetic renderings of ideas that Winnicott was to develop in his writing on infant development. He was intrigued by Wordsworth's use of the preverbal and the nonverbal, as in Wordworth's *Ode on the Intimations of Immortality*: "But for those first affections/Those shadowy recollections" (Hutchinson & De Selincourt, 1966).

Winnicott related strongly to Keats's poetry, which captured the uncertainties and doubts of the human experience while exploring the mysteries of the imagination.

The American transcendentalists also strongly influenced Winnicott's ideas, especially Ralph Waldo Emerson. In his essay *Self Reliance*, Emerson encourages the reader to be true to his own nature and intuition. While Emerson doesn't use the words "true self" there are strong parallels between that Winnicottian concept and Emerson's emphasis on the value of personal perception and expression. Emerson stressed the importance of being true to one's own individuality and shunning conformity. "Imitation is suicide," Emerson wrote (Bradley, Beatty, & Long, 1962).

Yet it was his contemporary, the poet T. S. Eliot, whose writing touched Winnicott in deeply personal ways, especially the poet's concern with time and timelessness. For Winnicott, Eliot was a fragmented modernist. It was Eliot's poetry that Winnicott asked his wife Clare to read to him at the end of his life. One can find in Eliot the same appreciation of paradox and "transitional space" that played such an important role in the development of Winnicott's thinking.

In this chapter are two poems and a letter young Winnicott sent to his mother. Also included is a poem by Masud Khan, who was a student, analysand, and editor of Winnicott. It is interesting to note that of the few extant poems by either man, each poem focuses on his relationship with his mother. A comparison of the two poems reveals the consequences of different forms of maternal failure and the child's effort to cope with it.

* * *

YOUNG DONALD'S LETTER TO HIS MOTHER

Donald Winnicott, age fourteen, wrote this letter to his mother when he was away at the Leys School in Cambridge in 1911. It shows his need, even in his early years, to enliven his depressed mother through play. One can infer from the letter what a burden it really was for him to be in that role, and what a task he had as a child.

My dearest Mother,

On September 2nd all true Scouts think of their mothers, since that was the birthday of Baden Powell's mother when she was alive. And so when you get this letter I shall be thinking of you in particular, and I only hope you will get it in the morning.

But to please me very much I must trouble you to do me a little favour. Before turning the page I want you to go up to my bedroom and in the right-hand cupboard find a small parcel. Now, have you opened it? Well, I hope you will like it. You can change it at Popham's if you don't. Only if you do so, you must ask to see No. 1, who knows about it.

I have had a ripping holiday, and I cannot thank you enough for all you have done and for your donation to the Scouts.

My home is a beautiful home and I only wish I could live up to it. However I will do my best and work hard and that's all I can do at present.

Give my love to the others; thank Dad for his game of billiards and V. and K. for being so nice and silly so as to make me laugh. But, it being Mother's Day, most love goes to you.

From your loving boy,
Donald

THE TREE

"The Tree" *was written by Donald Winnicott at age sixty-seven and is said to be about Winnicott's mother.*

When Winnicott wrote this poem in 1963 he sent it to his good friend James Britton, Clare Winnicott's brother, and enclosed this note: "Do you mind seeing this that hurt coming out of me? I think it had some thorns sticking out somehow. It's not happened to me before & I hope it doesn't again." In his book on Winnicott, Adam Phillips (1988) suggests that the poem's identification of Christ on the cross refers to the absence of the way the mother "holds" the child in her mind as well as her arms. It also seems to refer to the way children attempt to deal with the mother's depressed or withdrawn mood. The poem suggests that the form of deprivation, where the child is compelled to attempt to enliven an inaccessible mother, is at the cost of the child's spontaneous vitality. The tree of the title may refer to a special tree in the Winnicott family garden, where Winnicott nestled to do his homework before being sent off to boarding school. From this vantage point, we could speculate that it is a tree connected to maternal separation.

THE TREE
D. W. WINNICOTT

Someone touched the hem of my garment
Someone, someone, someone

I had much virtue to give
I was the source of virtue
    the grape of the vine of the wine

I could have loved a woman
          Mary, Mary, Mary
There was not time for loving
I must be about my father's business
There were publicans and sinners
The poor we had always with us
There were those sick with the palsy
    and the blind and the maimed
    and widows bereft and grieving
    women wailing for their children
    fathers with prodigal sons
    prostitutes drawing their own water
        from deep wells in the hot sun

Mother below is weeping
        weeping
        weeping
Thus I knew her

Once, stretched out on her lap
    as now on a dead tree
I learned to make her smile
      to stem her tears
      to undo her guilt
      to cure her inward death

To enliven her was my living

So she became wife, mother, home
The carpenter enjoyed his craft

Children came and loved and were loved
Suffer little children to come unto me

Now mother is weeping
She must weep

The sins of the whole world weigh less than this
        woman's heaviness

O Glastonbury

Must I bring even these thorns to flower?
        Even this dead tree to leaf?

How, in agony
Held by dead wood that has no need of me
    by the cruelty of the nail's hatred
                of gravity's inexorable and heartless pull
I thirst
No garment now
No hem to be touched
It is I who need virtue
Eloi, Eloi, lama sabachthani?

It is I who die
    I who die
    I die
    I

A POEM BY MASUD KHAN

Masud Khan was Winnicott's student, analysand, and editor. Below is a poem Khan wrote in 1963 about his own mother—the fourth wife of his father, who married her at age seventy-six. She was a courtesan who already had an illegitimate child, and was allegedly in her teens when they married. She was perceived by Khan as a simple woman, prone to "anxious chatter," who could not keep up with him. When he was seven years old, his mother went to visit her family in a village several hundred miles away, promising to return in thirty days. When a telegram arrived on the twenty-ninth day, announcing that she would be delayed, Masud's father raged and swore vengeance, terrorizing the entire household. When his mother finally returned, Masud refused to drive to the railway station to meet her. When she arrived at the house, he refused to greet her. "You have dishonoured my father and let me down," he told her. She slapped his face, for the first time ever, and he said that he never spoke to her again.

I CANNOT HEAR
MASUD KHAN

I cannot hear
I cannot hear you,
mother.
Not your wailing or chantings,
or the whispering of maids around you.
The dead leaves are crumpled
and stuffed in my ears.
I heard the shriek,
knew it was you,
killed it, mother.
My mad inconsolable mother.
I killed your voice insisting in my ears.

I cannot hear.
What I touch and see is mine,
mother,
and I cannot share.
I cannot hear.
Mother.
Mother.
Mother.

SLEEP

D. W. WINNICOTT

At the end of his life, Winnicott wrote the poem, "Sleep." Can it be about mortality? Or about the dream world, and the unconscious? Does it speak to the inner/outer world of intermediate space? Or about tapping into a source of endless creativity?

Let down your tap root
to the centre of your soul
Suck up the sap
from the infinite source
of your unconscious
And
Be evergreen.

References

1. Goldman, D. (1993). *In Search of the Real: The Origins and Originality of D. W. Winnicott.* Northvale, NJ: Jason Aronson.
2. Hutchinson, T., & De Selincourt, E. (Eds.) (1966). *William Wordsworth, Poetical Works.* London: Oxford University Press.
3. Bradley, S., Beatty, R. C., & Long, E. H. (Eds.) (1962). *Self Reliance,* by Ralph Waldo Emerson in *The American Tradition in Literature (Volume 1).* New York: W. W. Norton.
4. Phillips, A. (1988). *Winnicott.* Cambridge, MA: Harvard University Press.

CHAPTER TWELVE

Mothers of the Milky Way
Part One: poetry

This chapter is dedicated to our mothers and to the mothers in all of us.

Here we pay homage to the complex relationship we have with our mothers: Ma, Mommy, Mom, Mama—mothers here and mothers gone, those vanishing before our eyes and those who are mothers themselves. Here we celebrate and mourn. Part One consists of poetry; Part Two is a collection of creative nonfiction.

In these chapters we offer a glimpse into the complexities of mother love. Mothers who nurture and inspire and offer exuberance and joy and blessedness, protectors of the hearth and the children; who laugh together until we cry, in good times and hard times, the creator and the lion-hearted. There is also a glimpse of the mother of many shadows—mothers where boundaries blur, who disappoint, who colonise us, live through us, and don't see us, who neglect and abandon, who cause us pain and even hate.

This is about older mothers and young mothers and women about to become mothers, capturing the most simple, quiet moments and the most dramatic and passionate. Some of these pieces recall a time gone by. Others are very much in the present. Some describe a reversal of roles. We hear the bold voices of daughters and mothers, mothers and sons.

One woman said, "My mother is my soul mate. She did not influence me, but rather listened to me with deep empathic eyes. A current passing back and forth. Now that she isn't here I am bereft and adrift. She was my great love."

The therapist-contributors have told me how much they appreciate finding a home for some of their innermost thoughts and feelings, where their creative and analytic minds can be one. It does take courage. "We contain so much," one contributor said, "and we have long needed a venue for self-expression."

The contributors have all done enormous internal work on motherhood, work that is never truly complete. The poet, Christina Rossetti expressed it this way:

> Will the day's journey take the whole long day?
> From morn to night, my friend?

Some of these offerings, told with unflinching honesty, made me weep. Others made me smile, while others left me speechless with a deep sadness and pain. In the end, for all its mystery, all its complexity, we have a longing for unconditional mother love and for life's rhythm that beats in the maternal heart.

* * *

MOONSTONES
KATH BURLINSON, PhD

My mother's eyes are changing.
Once they were sapphires
Welcoming the day,
Reflecting and projecting
The sparkle of being
With a love so optimistic
I would feel shamed
By my bleary grunts,
Shuffling towards the kettle.

Now my mother's eyes are changing.
The sapphire's iridescent precision
Only occasional now,
A sudden blast of twinkle
Through the obstacles of age.
They are moonstones now,
My mother's eyes. The shimmer
A little milky, diffuse,
And she seems to look both farther off and
Farther in.

She sees a place that only she can see
A space where only she will go
Where none of us can follow
Not even with a cup of tea and a biscuit.
And where her sapphires shot me into consciousness,
Caught my numb soul and insisted on the beauty of morning,
Her moonstones gently show me
That she knows her own path into the mystery of night.

Kath Burlinson, PhD, is a UK-based theatre practitioner and founder of the Authentic Artist Collective. Previously she lectured in English & Drama at Southampton University and published on nineteenth-century women's writing, including *Christina Rossetti* (1998) in the series, *Writers & Their Work*.

THIS ONE
TERRANCE McLARNAN, MFT

This one
Sits very still
For days and days

This one
Watches traffic
For entertainment

This one
Lost
Her melody

This one
Can barely
Feed herself

This one
Sleeps &
Messes her pants

This one
Is not the
Momma I know

Yet,
This one's voice
Always … always
Turns my ear

Terrance McLarnan, MFT. I am/I was: field worker, paperboy, Little League umpire, tree planter, carpenter (power tools and mashed thumbs), dishwasher (professional), janitor (graveyard shift), gardener (roses), clown (but no fool), elevator machinist (assembled the damn things), analyst (of a number of things).

MY DEAD MOTHER LIVES INSIDE MY HEAD
MARGARET ALLAN, PsyD

My dead mother lives inside my head
She's not very big, she's not very dead
She has a way of feeding off my eyes
And nudges me at night with the sound of her cries.
But she doesn't make trouble in her little cocoon,
I've promised her the earth, I've promised her the moon,
If she's not there, well, what would I do,
We're so comfortable and cosy like a foot in a shoe.

Margaret Allan, PsyD, is a psychoanalyst living and working in Southern California. She has a particular interest in bringing the power of these dark arts out of the consulting room and to the people, in community based endeavors. Growing up in Sydney, Australia, she never planned to live anywhere else but was moved by love. She is part sea mammal who can't eat an apple without eating the core, something her mother taught her.

WAITING TO BECOME A FOSTER MOTHER
NAOMI SINGER, LMSW

Dear Child,

I have never met you but I know what you look like.
I've never heard you, but I know your voice.
I don't know your name, but I'm ready to call it.
To sing it. To rejoice it.
How strange that you are a mystery, but there's already a seat
for you.
A place for you in my home and in my pliable heart.
There is a nest
Built with books and stories and ice cream and cats.
All we need is you to come in.

Stranger than not knowing you (for you are, for now, a stranger)
Is that I don't know who I'll be when you're here.
Will I be NayNay or Mama or who knows what
I'll become.

I don't know. Who you will be, who I will be, or we.
But I know that there are seats for all of us. Here.
All we need is to climb in.

Naomi Singer, LMSW, is a geriatric social worker in New York whose parenting impulse, until now, has been enacted only on friends' and family's children, and her own cats. She is not a writer but was inspired to record these words for herself, to mark this moment of anticipation and not-knowing. While she and her husband, who live in Brooklyn, were waiting to become foster parents, she became pregnant and has since given birth to a baby boy.

day 56
CELESTE BIRKHOFER

life as I knew it changed in an instant
when I got the call you pray you'll never get
the words ripped through me clearing space for the unthinkable

tormented by a need to make sense of it
I keep revisiting my son's suffering
building a case for the part of him that saw no other way

it wasn't supposed to turn out like this
such enormous love and effort
should guarantee a different outcome

they tell me it won't always feel this way
but the ache in my heart
sets up what feels like permanent residence

even the good memories
are agonizing
reminders of what's absent and will never be again

gratitude for 27 precious years hovers in the background
a fragile competitor to indescribable sadness and a recurring protest
this cannot be

Celeste Birkhofer, PhD, PsyD, MFT, is a psychoanalyst in Menlo Park, California. She is a member of the Institute of Contemporary Psychoanalysis and teaches graduate seminars on psychoanalysis in Palo Alto and Los Angeles. She received the 2015 Stephen Mitchell Award for her paper, "Theoretical Diversity & Pluralism: Change, Challenges & Benefits."

INCONNU
KAREN HOPENWASSER, MD

When I was in college I received a letter from my mother asking me to please use punctuation in my letters to her, and ending with the ancient Greek aphorism, Know Thyself. I wrote this poem for her a number of years after she "crossed over."

Standing on the cutting edge the soles of my feet shred with
    every step.
You whisper into my ear from down the river, from the other side,
where I remember places I have never been, crossings I have
    never crossed,
in a language *you* spoke as a child.
You say, choose between the pain of knowing and the pain of
    not knowing.

When I was young you taught me how to find my way home.
From that day on, never have I been lost in the desire to be rescued.
Only my body remembers the yearning for contact,
that which remains unknown.

In memoriam I plant impatiens,
searching for another sort of home,
the place where a bell is ringing in the sky,
a single resonance to lift my spirit onto safe ground,
safe from the downstream current, safe from the crossing over.

Each time I visit you in the dark place I hear the nightingale
    from afar.
She sits on the limb of future time,
singing her bittersweet song:
te nosce, te nosce,
song to guide me safely home.

Karen Hopenwasser, MD, is an integrative psychiatrist in private practice in New York City and clinical associate professor of psychiatry at Weill Cornell Medicine. She is the author of many professional papers and book chapters on trauma, dissociation, and rhythmic attunement. Music and poetry have been and always will be enmeshed with her professional life.

A CHILD PRAYS
IGNATIUS KIM

My early memory
Kneeling at the cheap repro of
Mother Mary, desperately
Praying for your immortality
I couldn't stanch the tears

At barely four, I didn't know
Where such terror came from
My longing torn open
By a mother's brittle frailty, both
Cruel and tender

We expect such peach perfection
The succulent blush of an
Omni-mother
Who cannot be
Not even close

Who in turn falls, mauled
By the unreality of ideals
So lovingly budded
To full term, a mother's
Disappointment is savage

But the poison passes
To the child, kneeling in
Split terror
All love and hate
We struggled to part

At last
I now see you as your own
Person, your youth
I can picture
Not quite a stranger

Ignatius Kim is a psychodynamic psychotherapist in Tasmania, Australia, trained in the Conversational Model with a broad range of influences from contemporary psychoanalysis. He also works as a clinical nurse consultant in forensic mental health services.

SKY BLUE
ELAINE WELLS, MFT

If I could have been
the sky for you

as you are my nature
to have been nestled
in my darkness

knowing all the stars
surround you

and light your dreams
while you sleep in mine

when the sun gradually
opens me into light

I become blue
and all the colors

of your nature
are revealed to you

when you open
to morning light

Elaine Wells, MFT, practices psychoanalysis in San Francisco. She sees individuals, couples, and consults. She's a longtime member of a theoretical and case seminar, as well as a psychoanalytic writing group. She writes poetry, short stories, and is currently working on a film.

HAVE YOU EVER SWALLOWED A SPIDER?
RONALD RUSKIN, MD

Part One: Childhood

Have you ever swallowed a spider?
And felt its hairy legs
Trying to climb out of your throat?

What does a spider taste like?
It depends. Most of the time
You don't bother savouring the taste

Eight legs, 48 knees, hair, a bloated
    abdomen
A head with fangs and eight eyes,
Don't worry about bones—spiders
    have none.

Of course it was an accident,
The spider was hiding in my mother's
    milk,
I was a little kid; I never saw it.

Basically I trusted my mother,
I trusted my mother's breasts
I drank the milk and spider all up.

Yes, I know it was a long time ago,
But each day swallowing milk and
    spiders
Added up to one hell of a mess inside
    me.

I tell people that I have nothing
    against spiders,
But every few years I find them hiding
    in milk.

I mean if you can't trust milk, what is
    life about?

Part Two: Adolescence

I had to run away,
Far away you know,
Life is full of spiders and webs hiding
    in milk.

For years I was careful, because, to tell
    the truth
I craved the soft silk hammock feel
Of the web and how it held me.

Webs encircle and bind you,
You sort of feel safe,
You can't ever be sure, so you leave.

Part Three: Adulthood

My analyst told me to lie down on the
    couch
For a while everything was fine, like
    a hammock
I felt safe until the analyst turned into
    a spider.

I hate to tell you, there is no happy
    ending,
Sometimes the analyst is just an
    analyst,
Sometimes the analyst is a spider, just
    like me.

Ronald Ruskin, MD, is psychiatrist-director at Mount Sinai Hospital, associate professor at University of Toronto, and training analyst on the faculty at Toronto Psychoanalytic Society and Toronto Institute for Contemporary Psychoanalysis. Ron has published short stories, poems, a medical thriller, and a comic medical novel, *The Analyst Who Laughed to Death* (Karnac, 2016).

CHAPTER THIRTEEN

Mothers of the Milky Way
Part Two: creative nonfiction

Mothers of song, mothers of trees, and mothers of thunder. Here, we continue exploring the complex relationships we have with our mothers through an intimate collection of creative nonfiction. We offer a second glimpse into the complexities of mother love, the nurturing mothers and the mother of many shadows— those who disappoint, neglect, and abandon, who cause us pain and even hate. The stories are filled with delight and with sorrow. They capture mothers of all ages. The words evoke simple and peaceful moments, as well as the most startling and powerful.

I recently read an anonymous quote on this theme that touched me. It evokes the sense memories that a good-enough mother can offer— though, as many of these contributions suggest, some mothers fall very short. "Your mother is always with you. She is the whisper of the leaves as you walk down the street. She is the smell of certain foods you remember, the fragrance of life itself. She is the cool hand on your brow when you're not feeling well. She's your breath in the air on a cold winter's day. Your mother lives inside your laughter. She's the place you came from, your first home. She is your first love, your first friend, even your first enemy. But nothing on earth can separate you—not time, not space, not even death."

The following unforgettable portraits of mothers have affected me deeply. Perhaps they will affect you as well.

* * *

A BRAND OF HOME
ANONYMOUS, PhD

There is something I have needed to write about for some time. I have felt its presence in me, pressing to be formed. It is something my father told me many years ago, very late in his life and very late in mine. This thing my father told me has grown gigantic in my mind. I have wrapped myself around it and made it home.

This thing my father told me late in both our lives is that when I was an infant he walked into my room, with the pretty pink rose wallpaper and little lambs blanket and saw my mother hoisting me high above her head, shaking me and shrieking as she thrust me up and down with all the rage and power all who knew her knew.

I knew too, of course. It happened most days. But I never thought before it might have happened as a baby.

I think I've wrapped around this for its power to explain, explain the inexplicable of the pain in which I live, the pain in which I have lived all of my life. When you are a baby and your mother screams at you, it puts a brand of pain in you that takes on its own life. It becomes life. It becomes home.

When pain like this is put in you so early in your life, are you doomed to have it the rest of your life? Does it infuse into your being and become who you are? Do you wrap yourself around it and make it your first love?

There was another brand of pain though, a brand, I think, more deep, a second brand of pain that my mother held for me. It was when I came to realize in a place beyond escape that the mother I knew hated me, also did not love me.

I came to this as truth in the years before the end, when the lumps grew everywhere and her skin went yellow, and she knew for years there was no chance she would survive, and she not once said good-bye to me nor thought to leave a note. She not once did one thing that showed she thought of me at all. In this my mother showed me I meant exactly nothing to her, and then my mother left me, then my mother died.

This is a wound that does not heal. This is a wound that brands. When the fear she did not love me entered into certainty, the screams of pain inside me made me long for her screams back.

I see children every day, in the store, on the street, in the mall, and sometimes they look up at me, little faces reading mine. In that fleeting moment when so much goes on between us, I hold their little selves close to me. I love them in my glance. Somehow, I know how.

I see adults every day, in the store, on the street, in the mall, and I see those same little faces looking back at me. We are all little children throughout all our lives. I am still that baby whose mother screamed at her. I am still that fourteen year old whose mother died silent. I am still all ages. We are all all ages.

In moments, I have wished for death over life with this pain. I have wanted to kill the mother I keep alive by living in it. Today I feel some peace, some sense it can be borne. I see leaving it and her as the work of this life for me.

As I have done this work, much life has entered in. It is joyous, this aliveness, the moments that it's here. It makes me think aliveness is what joy is made up of.

One thing though still eludes me, one thing remains interred: love lies still unreclaimable from the grave she and I placed it in. I remain as I was, unloved and untouched and desperate for what is not there for me. It is the wound I cannot heal. The aliveness I cannot allow. The attachment I cannot mourn. I am a baby branded forever as one who is not loved. I cannot find, and I cannot leave home.

Anonymous, PhD, is a psychoanalyst in full-time private practice. She has written anonymously to protect her confidentiality for practice reasons. The author "hopes there might be some readers who relate to her story and in whose minds it might find a home."

MY THREE MOTHERS
MARY LIBBEY, PhD

A beautiful nineteen-year-old girl married a handsome military officer six years her senior, an "officer and a gentleman." Charming and flirtatious, she was favored by everyone, adored by her own father, and adored by mine. To me too, when I was little, she was a wondrous mix of Snow White, a quiet Geisha, and the mother played by Jane Wyatt in the Fifties TV show, *Father Knows Best*.

Without planning, she gave birth to four children in her first five years of marriage. As one of those young children, I was often told that I was lucky to have such a young and beautiful mother. I remember not understanding why this made me lucky. Mostly, I remember feeling love and longing toward her. With long curly brown hair framing twinkling light blue eyes, rosy cheeks, and an angelic smile, she was visually soothing—like white linen, like porcelain, like a delicately flowered pillow. Her disposition was calm and quiet, and she seemed knowing. As a young child, wherever she was in the house, I would find her. I would sit down and talk to her endlessly while she quietly listened. I became determined to be like her, both for myself as well as for her approval. She was my ideal.

I had no way of knowing then that she was a natural introvert. I did not know that she felt un-mothered by her own mother, parented more by her father for whom she was the favorite. I always knew she loved my father, but it took me a long time to pick up on an edge of bitterness she also felt toward him for his expectations of her. I could never have known then that she had never wanted children. "Are you sure you do?—I didn't." I didn't know until she told me recently that she felt that the best years of her life had been her teenage years, at home with her own large family, at long dinners filled with laughter, big birthday parties, and picnics in the back yard to which she often brought her enamored dates.

Knowing none of these things, I loved my mother as she appeared— quiet and ladylike. Someone to "behave" around. Someone's good graces to win. Her good behavior was its own command for my good behavior.

As my latency years became adolescence, I changed and my mother changed. I was not turning out to be a "lady." Rather, I pushed for things for myself. I was extremely talkative, emotional, and highly reactive.

I complained. I talked with my hands. In my process of becoming, my mother became my critic.

Along the way, I also realized that, without intending to, I made her laugh. Initially I remember feeling troubled that she laughed when I slammed my fingers in the car door, and another time when I walked through a screen door, getting scratched up in the process. Happily, I discovered that I could intentionally make her laugh, and I became the family comedian. Unfortunately, however, over time her criticalness, amusement, and eventually her mocking sarcasm became unpredictably interwoven and interchangeable, and I came to know shame around her.

By the time I finished college, I was aware that I had two mothers, a calm charming one and a demeaning one. But no one else seemed to notice, much less confirm, this duality. For years during my young adulthood, I asked myself: which one was the real her? Was I just imagining her changeability? Was it only with me, or did she do it with everyone?

Now well into adulthood, I have the experience of a third mother. As the decades have passed, I realize that in her own experience of herself she is still a girl. I know now that her own mother's mothering left off at making sure she secured a husband. Her mother didn't guide her into womanhood or motherhood, or any kind of strong sense of self, but rather enjoyed her own life's little pleasures way too much. I know now that my mother's watchful criticalness is both a compensation for, as well as projection of, her own sense of inadequacy when she faces something she can't manage. I know now that my mother is quiet, not only because she is a private, self-sufficient introvert—but also because she is prone to feeling shame herself, as is anyone who hides their feelings with authoritativeness and a cover of self-sufficiency. I know now that when her wisecracks come my way, it is not only because she disapproves of me, which she does, but because I am momentarily slotted in her mind alongside her self-involved mother. And I know this is one version of the way mothers and daughters alternate roles throughout life.

Everyone loves their mother of origin, even when they don't consciously. I know a woman who always said she hated her mother, but on her mother's deathbed yelled at her for not loving her, just like the Tom Cruise character in the movie *Magnolia* yelled at his father on his deathbed: "I hate you! You should have been nicer to me!" And then sobbed, "I love you, I love you."

Freud told us that love for one's mother is one's first love, and that subsequent loves are based on that first love. I believe this, but I also believe that love for one's actual mother persists for a lifetime, and may or may not evolve. She is the first experience of love, even if memories of those earliest experiences of love cannot be felt anymore. It is the rare person who gives up altogether on one's real life mother. By and large, she will remain in dreams, self-perceptions, and object choices.

My mother still admonishes me out of the blue. But I know now that she does not know how to offer empathy or support because she never received it. While she and I now treat each other politely and kindly—real responses to each other not part of our interactions—I understand that it is the best we can do. She does not fault me as much as she used to, but she will if I am myself, and I will feel exposed. I do not challenge her because I know she too will feel the sudden pain that shame entails.

In the beginning and in the end, my mother's ideal self is a good girl. Despite the tremendous disparities in our characters and personalities and the emotional distance between us, I realize that I still deeply love the girl who was such sweet solace in my early years. Still mentally sharp at ninety-two, when she falls or is rushed to the hospital, I feel terrified and frightened of losing her. I know at these times that she feels like a frightened and helpless girl, even though she doesn't show it. And I am highly aware of my love for this girl whom I call *Mother*.

Mary Libbey, PhD, is a member of the faculty and a supervisor at the NYU Postdoctoral Program in Psychoanalysis and at IPTAR. She teaches courses on narcissism and shame, and writes about the personal experience of doing psychoanalytic work. She is in private practice in Manhattan, and also makes intricately beaded jewelry.

EMILY
ELIZABETH HOWELL, PhD

On the other end of the phone with me, she was swallowing her last breaths, struggling to get words out as her lungs were filling with fluid. But she tried to speak with her gurgled, badly distorted words that sounded as if they were coming through water—which in fact they were. In these last moments of her life, my mother reappeared as a mother and as a lucid person, even through her garbled speech. She said to me two things that she had never said to me before. She said, "I love you. I am so proud of you." Then she could no longer talk. I couldn't hear her breathing anymore.

Never before had she told me she was proud of me. I was, of course, touched by what she said, and I deeply appreciated her honoring me with her last words. I so appreciated how in her last moments she was finally able to come out of the self-absorption that had overcome her for the past thirty years, and to show up as a real person with feelings and thoughts about me. For the first time I could remember, I felt like there was an "us." I cried with a strange mix of gratitude and sorrow for the rest of the day.

I felt that she had redeemed herself, that she had brought herself back to life in those, her last dying moments. I felt that the person she had once been was here again, that her lost mind, that she had both carelessly given away but that also had been wrongfully stolen from her, had finally returned to her.

I was grateful and glad for her. Even though I cried deeply, I was not deeply moved in a transformative way for myself. I deeply, deeply appreciated her last words, that they were her last words, that they were to me, and that they were words of love, but while her words moved me, they did not change me; they did not penetrate my core.

Elizabeth Howell, PhD, has written extensively and lectured nationally and internationally on various aspects of trauma and dissociation, as well as on gender and trauma/dissociation. She coedited with Sheldon Itzkowitz, *The Dissociative Mind in Psychoanalysis: Understanding and Working With Trauma*. She grew up in Dallas, Texas, and transplanted to New York City for college.

ON BECOMING THE TOOTH FAIRY
RACHEL KARLINER, PhD

As a mother of young children, I enjoyed the small, playful delights that came with the job, including being the tooth fairy. At night, I got to embody the mysterious character who plays with the child's connection to a magical world. Slipping back into the role of mother in the morning, I loved seeing the excitement and puzzlement on my children's faces when they found treasure under their pillows. I learned that the tooth fairy, like all transitional objects, can help with questions about reality and fantasy—can something be real and imagined all at once? And I discovered that because a child forms a relationship with the tooth fairy over many years, this imagined being may help with the complicated process of growing up.

My son's first tooth had to be pulled by the dentist. That night, he wrote a detailed note to the tooth fairy, explaining the ordeal and asking for something special in return, thus beginning our family tradition. By the time he was eight, he needed something different. Confronting me, he said, "Mom, you and I both know that *you* are the tooth fairy." As both prosecutor and judge, he was not letting me off the hook.

Was I the tooth fairy if he didn't believe anymore? And should I stop performing my tooth fairy duties if I had been discovered? Silently creeping into my child's room, retrieving his baby tooth from under his heavily sleeping head, replacing it with some treasure ... perhaps, I thought, my son simply needed a bit of consensual reality—reassurance—as he went on being a child. Despite his discovery, I continued to leave him treasure for some time. The spell was broken, but the ritual continued until it simply faded away.

My daughter, then age five, had been engaging in a lively correspondence with the tooth fairy for a year already. In her early notes, she identified herself as her brother's sister, as though locating herself in the tooth fairy's mind. Over time, the notes became letters, signed with her own name, and filled with questions about the tooth fairy's life and history. In my responses, composed in curlicue writing late at night after everyone was sleeping, I began to dream up a world, speaking to the wonderings of a little girl.

Age five: "Dear The Tooth Fairy, I lost my tooth ... I have a question for you. How do you know if somebody lost a tooth?" Response:

"I know when a breeze blows across my nose, and I follow that small, tiny breeze to a sleeping child's mouth to see a new space."

Age seven: "Dear The Tooth Fairy, this is my eighth tooth, one week and five days before I turn seven. I was brushing my teeth when it came out. Do you mind if you write me a little book called 'A Tooth Fairy's Life,' by The Tooth Fairy?" Response: "A little book that begins, "I was born in a small fairy town called Glen Aerie, deep in the forested mountains of Green Fernland, far, far away …"

Green Fernland? I had never imagined such a place before! What was happening? Late at night, charmed by my daughter's earnest belief, I was becoming *her* tooth fairy.

Soon her letters shifted in tone. They began to focus on our relationship and its limitations. I heard a poignant wish for more contact, accompanying an emergent awareness about the losses involved in growing up. I heard questions about my powers as a magical being. As the tooth fairy, I wanted to find a way to gently keep my distance while magically staying connected. As my daughter's mother, I began to realize that the tooth fairy letters were helping us to manage our feelings about separating. Now, on more familiar terms, she addressed the letters simply to "tooth fairy," lower case.

"Dear tooth fairy, if I write a letter to you when I haven't lost a tooth, would you know that I wrote to you? Is it possible that we could become pen pals? Could we keep in touch?" Response: "I would love to keep in touch with you, but alas, I only know to come when a child has lost a tooth. Perhaps, together, we can think of a sign or a message that would reach me."

"Dear tooth fairy, why can I not see you? Why am I not allowed? I was wondering if you could draw me a self-portrait?" Response (with accompanying self portrait): "To answer why you cannot see me, it is part of the ancient fairy magic that the tooth fairy becomes invisible if a child awakens, so as not to frighten her. But you might feel the flutter of my wings one night, brushing against your cheek."

Finally, at age ten, my daughter lost a tooth at sleep-away camp. She couldn't help but question the tooth fairy's existence when she didn't get a response until visiting weekend. "Mom?" she asked, "*are* you the tooth fairy?" And before I could answer, "Don't tell me! Don't tell me until I've lost my last tooth!" I was spared having to confront the reality that my son had so clearly needed. By knowing and needing not to know at the same time, my daughter granted both of us the transitional space to keep the tooth fairy alive.

During this period, her questions were incisive and specific:

Age ten: "Dear tooth fairy, did a human or fairy or other creature come to you when you lost your teeth? What made you decide to be a TOOTH FAIRY? Or were you born into the tooth fairy lifestyle? I wish I could meet you but I know it's against the 'rules.'"

Age eleven: "Dear tooth fairy, how many kids exactly are you the tooth fairy for at one time? And how does *which* tooth fairy get assigned to *which* kid? Is your name actually 'THE TOOTH FAIRY?'"

Under the surface, I heard her asking how the world works, how she could identify with the tooth fairy and see her as a separate person all at once. On a deeper level, I heard her asking how mothers and children "find" each other, and how a mother keeps her child or children in mind.

When my daughter lost her last tooth, she looked at me knowingly. "Mom, I realized something. Just because *you* are the tooth fairy, it doesn't mean the tooth fairy isn't real." Through our letters, I had become the tooth fairy for my daughter, real in both of our minds. While my son needed to acknowledge the difference between fantasy and reality in order to go on being, my daughter needed to suspend this acknowledgement for a time, using the quasi-magical world we had created to navigate her childhood.

Rachel Karliner, PhD, is a clinical psychologist and a candidate at the NYU Postdoctoral Program in Psychotherapy and Psychoanalysis. She has written and presented on symbolization in psychoanalytic treatment, the parent–child relationship, and psychoanalytic play therapy. She is in private practice in New York City.

A ONE-OF-A-KIND MOTHER
JILL CHODER-GOLDMAN, LCSW

Just the word "Mother" is complicated in itself. Add relationships with mothers, well that's a whole different story. I had a mother and now I am a mother and although it's a very different relationship it's still complex and full of mistakes, albeit different from the ones my mother made.

My mother was a character, a cigarette smoking, poker playing, outspoken, judgmental hard-ass and loving mother. There was nothing she wouldn't do for me. I was her everything and I mean everything. She lived through me and because I came out of her womb singing like Ethel Merman and tap dancing like Fred Astaire, she was in heaven.

Here was her way out … or her way in … to show business and a glamorous life. Fortunately I was a great candidate because I was born to entertain so it was a "perfect fit," at least for awhile.

Here is just one example of what my mother was willing to do. When I was just twelve years old she took me along with my best friend Beverly to New York to see a Broadway show. By then I had already done shows in summer stock and performed in the Catskills but not yet on Broadway. While we were sitting in the first row of the mezzanine watching *Bye Bye Birdie*, I can remember poking my mom and whispering, "I want to be in this show and I want to play that part." I guess she heard me because as we were on our way back to Squirrel Hill in Pittsburgh, my mother just happened to have an 8 × 10 glossy of me along with my resume, which she dropped off at the stage door of the Shubert Theatre before heading home. Crazy, huh, but that was my mother. She wasn't quite Mama Rose, but she was a close second.

Surprising to say, the stage manager of *Bye Bye Birdie* called my mother in Pittsburgh one night while I was doing my homework in the kitchen asking if she would bring me to NY for an audition. They were casting for replacements and he thought I might be right for the show based on my picture. Well of course my mother said "yes." No, let me tell the truth, she practically yelled into the phone, "Of course we can, what time do you need us there"?

Three days later, we got on a Greyhound bus for New York, stayed at the YWCA on 8th Avenue, and showed up at the Shubert Theatre the next morning at 10 a.m.

For the next day and a half I went through hours of singing and dancing on the stage of the Shubert Theatre where eliminations were being made all day long, while my mother was waiting in the backstage area ALL DAY LONG [until they politely asked her to leave]. Now, in her defense, remember I was only twelve years old.

When the day was over, I was left standing and told to come back the next morning for more of the same. My mother was beside herself and I was pretty excited as well. By the end of the next day, I got the job. She was really excited! That was the beginning of a very long career in the theater with my mother by my side.

She loved the glamour and she was there for the tears and rejections as well. She loved all of it, so much so that when I changed careers after having my own daughter she was never the same.

What happened to her little girl with all this talent going to waste, she thought? She couldn't understand that maybe I had changed after having my own daughter. That maybe I had had enough of the glamour, lights, and applause.

That was always sad to me, because it felt like her love was conditional based on my success in show business. I know she was proud of my new accomplishments but to her they just weren't as glamorous. She just couldn't applaud my search for knowledge, for change, and my desire to help others.

As far as me becoming a psychoanalyst? She always referred to my patients as my "customers."

Jill Choder-Goldman, LCSW, is the interview editor of *Psychoanalytic Perspectives* and a psychoanalyst/psychotherapist. She received her undergraduate and graduate degrees from NYU and her postgraduate psychoanalytic and supervisory training from the National Institute for the Psychotherapies, where she is now a clinical supervisor and advisor. She also has a private practice in New York City, treating individuals, couples, and groups.

BROKEN BARRIERS
LEAH VOLKOW

As the door opens, the daughter is struck by the sight of elderly people sitting in rows watching TV. She sees her mother looking towards her, waving her hands, calling her name and shouting "This is my daughter!"

Born in Warsaw in 1929, she experienced human cruelty, the disappearance of her family, deportations to concentration camps. All that culminated in a "death march" that she survived. Returning to "ordinary life," still a young girl, she fell in love with a rich, handsome, educated man who offered her wonderful opportunities. She broke off with him, telling herself that his father was not a "real Jew" and now after the Holocaust she couldn't allow herself to flee the Jewish fate. But she also feared that being in love might bring to the fore the emotions she had done her utmost to suppress. She gave little thought to such questions as what having a life of her own would mean, what narrative would guide her life, what she would do with the freedom to make choices.

A few years later, beginning again in Israel, the only place she could think of to live her life, she met a survivor who had also come "from there." It was not love, just a mutual agreement to start a family, mainly to prove to the Nazis they had failed to annihilate all the Jews. The wedding ceremony was modest, attended by some friends and family. When, ten months later, she gave birth to her daughter, her wish to have something of her own came true; she may also have been hoping that having a child would ease the never-ending pain. She breastfed her baby, but eight months later, she was surprised and disappointed to find herself pregnant again: nursing her infant had not protected her. She stopped abruptly and a month later, her daughter was toilet trained.

But to the mother's surprise, the child, like all children, had an agenda of her own. She fled from the room when her mother showed her pictures of the death camps—the hills of ashes, the piles of shoes, the dead bodies. The mother talked about "those times," but she reacted by sealing herself off to the meaning of the pictures and the emotions they evoked. She did her best to avoid seeing the pictures or hearing the stories. And always she heard her mother's voice saying: "You selfish creature."

The daughter always felt she was disappointing her mother, who wanted to fill the void, ease the pain by sharing her horrible stories. But she was reluctant to listen, intuitively knowing that refusing to do so was the best way for her to survive, to have an emotional and social life of her own. She was rarely hugged or caressed. She never missed it as a child, not knowing it was an option in mother–daughter relations, only realizing it when she herself became a mother.

When her first child was born, "coincidentally," on the eve of Holocaust Memorial Day, her mother felt there was nothing surprising about it: "That's how it ought to be in our family," she said. Now a grandmother, she offered to stay with her daughter the first night home with her three-day-old son. He cried a lot, and his mother hugged and comforted him. But then her mother intervened, firmly saying: "Don't let him be dependent on you, don't spoil him." Then it hit her like a bolt of lightning. The mother–daughter story became clear.

Now at the age of eighty-five, deep in a state of dementia, she no longer remembers anything about the Holocaust. She does not remember her late husband, her beloved grandchildren. None of her great intellectual abilities remain.

Now that her personality has collapsed, there are no more barriers to feelings. No more need to detach herself emotionally to avoid some future catastrophe. The only person she recognizes now and calls by name is her daughter. Every week they spend a few hours together— walking, singing, hugging. The mother tells her how much she loves her, needs her, how important she is to her life. And the daughter accepts this with compassion.

Leah Volkow is a clinical social worker, certified therapist, and supervisor in family and marriage therapy, sex therapy, and gerontology, who works at a private clinic in Ra'anana, Israel. She has dealt with death and life throughout her personal and professional life. She is happy to find life intriguing and surprising.

HOW TO BE YOUR MOTHER
TYIA GRANGE ISAACSON, LCSW

You are newly seven. We are at a children's festival waiting in line at a food truck. You, your brother, and your father run around on the lush grass nearby, and you check back six times asking if the food is ready. When at last I reach the front of the line, you are standing next to me as I order. "I'll have ..." But the order-taker interjects: "Be with you in one moment." I grit my teeth, inhale sharply, and tussle your hair. You watch the order-taker help the cooks; your eyes follow her as she changes the oil in the sweet potato fryer and restocks the all-natural soda and the biodegradable forks, arranging them just so. She disappears for a minute. Suddenly, she reappears at the counter and announces, "We are out of hot dogs."

You hear my too-loud voice snarl. "Are you kidding me? I have been standing in line for forty-five minutes, and now you ran out of hot dogs?"

Silence. You watch the cooks inside the truck stop their burger flipping to gape at your mother, this harried woman angry over hot dogs. You hear me rant on. "Didn't you know you were running low before just ... just springing it on us? It's only noon, and here you are at a children's event. It's a universal rule that the one item all children will eat is a hot dog!"

You catch my arm as we walk away. "Mom," you say, "what if I grow up and work there, and you don't recognize me? Would you say the same thing to me if I made that mistake?" You squint up at me as I mumble something about teaching you to make better choices.

You run ahead to watch the show. Suspended in midair, trapeze artists flip and twist in smashing single-arm holds. There's a children's band, and the lead singer is wearing a chicken mask. Your request to purchase overpriced maracas is turned down, and we bang on tables instead. You dance in the sun, and all the while your words stay with me.

That night, as I tuck you into bed I say, "I have been thinking about your question—how you asked if I would be angry at you if you made a mistake and I didn't recognize you. I am so glad you asked me that." A faint ripple of a smile tugs at the corner of your mouth. Your steady, round blue eyes with impossible lashes looking into mine. "I learn a lot from you," I say.

"That sweaty order-taker in her burger joint paper hat is somebody's daughter. Your seven-year-old soul was tugging on my busy arm asking me to stop. Asking me to see."

Snuggled into your bed, overflowing with stuffed animals, your favorite dog clutched in your arms, there is hardly any room. Yet I want to make some space. I want to tell you how profound you are, how humble I feel. How much you teach me about how to be a mother. Your mother. How I learn from you how to be a decent person in this world, and what this world looks like through your eyes. How, when I am paying attention, you teach me everything I need to know.

Tyia Grange Isaacson, LCSW, has a psychotherapy practice in the San Francisco Bay Area. She received a BA in creative writing and is earning her PhD from the Institute of Contemporary Psychoanalysis. She can also be found waiting patiently in long food truck lines.

CHAPTER FOURTEEN

Art brut—outsider art

I have long been interested in "outsider art", or *art brut* (raw, unrefined art)—work by self-taught creators who might be patients in a psychiatric hospital, or physically disabled, or people on the fringe whose lifestyle does not meet societal expectations—all of whom work unmindful of public esteem and the accepted traditions of art. The very first collection of outsider art was assembled by the French painter and sculptor Jean Dubuffet in 1945 and now numbers 60,000 works at a museum in Lausanne, Switzerland.

On a lovely spring day in Paris in 2003, walking through the Tuileries, I passed the Jeu de Paume Museum and went in to an exhibit of *art brut*, called "La Clé des Champs"—a metaphor for freedom. It turned out to be one of the most exciting and original art exhibits I had ever seen. Most interesting was the work of Aloise Corbaz, who had been institutionalized at La Rosière Asylum in Gimel, Switzerland for forty-four years until her death. She divided her schedule between drawing and ironing. She did her drawing in secret, sometimes using the sap of petals, crunched leaves, and toothpaste. But she never seemed to finish her ironing. All this attests to the transcendent power of the creative spirit.

Recently, I learned that Samantha Mitchell works with outsider artists at the Center for Creative Works in Philadelphia. We met on a Sunday morning at the Outsider Art Fair in Chelsea, in downtown New York, and she showed me this world through her eyes. Then, over lunch, she spoke about her fascinating work and I invited her to "curate" the creative section of the winter 2016 issue of the journal.

Samantha is the daughter of two psychoanalysts, Margaret Black Mitchell and Stephen Mitchell. She studied painting and Russian literature at Oberlin College, and received her MFA in painting from Pennsylvania Academy of Fine Arts. Her interest now is in drawing and printmaking.

Here is Samantha Dylan Mitchell, and her impressive work with outsider artists.

* * *

OUTSIDER ARTISTS AT WORK
SAMANTHA DYLAN MITCHELL

The Center for Creative Works is an art studio for adults with developmental disabilities just outside of Philadelphia. None of the art staff—who are the primary source of services, contact, and interaction for CCW participants—have training in psychology or social work. We are not tasked with therapy or rehabilitation, and thus none of us has been trained on the complexities of the diagnoses of participants. Instead, the point of interactive contact is based solely in interpersonal engagement, and in visual art.

I started working at CCW in the summer of 2012, after completing an MFA in painting. What we know of the people we work with is mostly from what we experience first-hand, uninformed by medical histories, preconceived ideas about mental illness and developmental disability, or a focus on fixing perceived problems. Instead, we learn to adapt and develop in conjunction with the participating artists. With art as a conduit for communication, our relationships and experiences of each other are based in visual interpretation and approach to material. The artwork that emerges from this environment is exciting, and entirely unique. Without formal aesthetic training, and oftentimes without a preconceived idea of what an artist must be, creation comes from a fluid transfer of impulse to action.

The field of outsider art has developed since the early twentieth century, when psychologists and artists became interested in artwork created by psychiatric patients. At present, "outsider" can be meant to include folk artists, self-taught artists, mentally ill artists, developmentally disabled artists, physically disabled artists, and untrained artists. Only recently has the conversation tentatively turned toward the idea of supporting living artists. Although the field of outsider art collection is rapidly becoming mainstream, facilities and programs to provide support for these artists are still relatively unknown and unsupported.

The art studio model that CCW is loosely based upon was developed by Florence Ludins-Katz and Elias Katz in 1983 at a San Francisco program called Creativity Explored. With a focus on personal development and growth through artistic expression, the program was the first to focus exclusively on the art of adults with developmental disabilities.

Many artists come to CCW with an independent practice fully developed, incorporating new materials as they wish. Others have had no exposure to art-making at all, and suddenly begin to create, forming a rich, expressive visual world.

Samantha Dylan Mitchell is an artist and writer, born to a family of psychoanalysts in New York City. She lives and works in Philadelphia.

ARTISTS

Jenny Garrity (b. 1976)

On any given day, Jenny Garrity will invariably be found drawing, seated with her nose so close to the surface of the page it seems as if she herself is emerging from it, part of the family of gnome-like figures she creates. With delicate, hair-thin lines, forms develop from the accumulation of mark, each topped with a domed, bald head and faint facial features, full of expressive force. In her own private, self-contained way, Garrity has conversations with these little communities she creates, often seeming to chat with them while they come to life, populating her page. Although Garrity is often nonverbal, she communicates richly through her sensitive, complex drawings.

Untitled, ink on paper, 2015.

Untitled, graphite on paper, 2015.

Owen Ahearn-Browning (b. 1992)

I love doing art about different places like that place called Cynwyd Elementary School that is near the middle school I went to for three years but the elementary school I was at for only one year only for a little while.

And my artwork is also on the fact that I have always loved being a free and energized man.

I think it's about time I enjoyed swimming in the Lower Merion High School Pool when the Chestnut Hill College Pool is gone and another thing I do art on is the different foods I still eat sometimes like chocolates or pizza I mean any of that and I also think that it's about time I wrote about basketball at Baldwin and the Upper Dublin Swimming Place on Saturday.

I think I need to do more artwork on different old times so any way that is all so anyway thank you again for all your time and okay both ciao and bye.

With a serious interest in storytelling and time-based perspective, Owen Ahearn-Browning creates through singing, performance art, writing, comic book-making, and drawing. His narrative thread spans time and space, pulling content from television and his own childhood with equally powerful immediacy and sense of ownership. With these cryptic, humorous drawings on note cards, a fluid feeling of connective understanding binds the viewer immediately to the work. Deceptively simple statements of objective truths are both ironic and deeply sincere. Ahearn-Browning's *Book about Furniture* was recently published for the Philadelphia Art Book Fair.

This is called an arm chair, ink on paper, 2016.

This is called a magnifying glass, which is also called something you can see out of, ink on paper, 2016.

This is called a raspberry pie, ink on paper, 2016.

This is called a bee and bee's are very dangerous because they sting which luckily still hasn't happened to me yet but they sting, ink on paper, 2016.

Mary T. Bevlock (b. 1968)

Make a picture in your mind of who you want to come to your house and to your dining room. It's like Thanksgiving, you're sitting at a table, and you can imagine who you want to come to your house and have dinner. A few of my family, Maurice Benard, my cousin Sally Jeffries, Carmine on "Laverne and Shirley." Picasso. Van Gogh.

My inspiration comes from books, shapes, my religion, and celebrities. My favorite material is colored pencils because none of the colors are alike, it feels like butter, with brighter colors. I like to blend because I get more colors that way. It feels great, wonderful, to make artwork, warm and happy feelings. So ... magic. Magical. I like response to my paintings, from anybody, that feels really good.

Mary Bevlock's dedication and focus on her vocation as an artist is inspiring and rare. She takes a systematic approach to her work in the studio, working with a well-tended tackle box of supplies and images collected over many years of use. With her passion for characters—both real and fictionalized—and an interest in portraiture, Bevlock develops a range of irreverent figures through a combination of focused attention to detail and a wild love of bold color and shape. *Clown* was recently exhibited in Cork, Ireland.

Clown, watercolor on paper, 2015.

Paige Donovan (b. 1991)

Dots and circles. Details. Straight lines. I like them because they're different, they pop into my brain and then I know everything about the painting.

I like painting landscapes. It reminds me of going outside in the summertime, and all the different leaves. There's deer behind our house, they came out of nowhere. There were two or three of them.

Over the past four years, Paige Donovan has developed a fascinating, original style of mark-making, first in acrylic paint and most recently in calligraphy ink. *Volcano vs. Jack Skeleton* is Donovan's first ink composition, and began as a response drawing to a figurative Henry Miller sculpture. By breaking the sculpture's areas of light and shadow into discrete shapes, the artist creates an abstracted mound, textured by a variety of distinct, cumulative marks. Donovan's vocabulary of mark comes from a desire to invent new and different ways of manipulating her materials, as well as an almost meditative approach to her art practice, which she continues to hone and develop every day. Donovan's work has been featured at several Philadelphia galleries, including Fleisher/Ollman, FJORD, and Pageant: Soloveev.

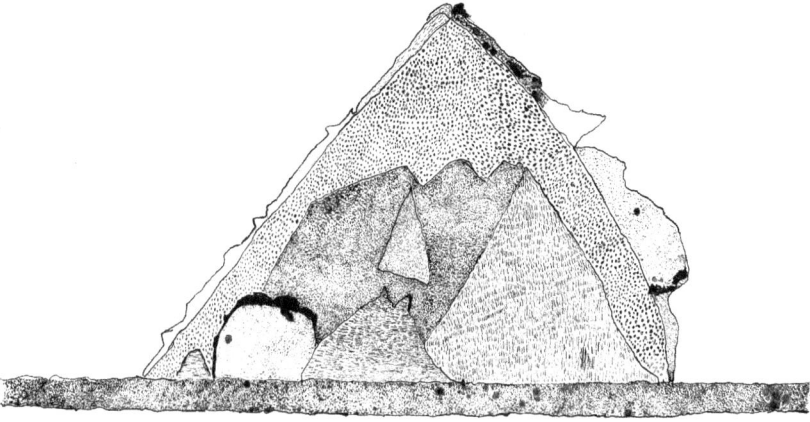

Volcano vs. Jack Skeleton, ink on paper, 2014.

CHAPTER FIFTEEN

Strong women's voices

The eight women writers featured in this chapter continue the great tradition of strong women's voices. Their writing is tough, blunt, and emotionally charged as they reflect on their life experiences from a feminine perspective, struggling against convention to liberate themselves. Simone de Beauvoir, the mother of feminism, knew about writing. She wrote about her life ceaselessly—in letters, diaries, articles for the journal she edited, four autobiographies, and several novels. She broke though gender roles and believed that women are made and not born. She didn't concern herself with pleasing others or being liked. She was bold and audacious.

Do women write in a different voice than men? Sometimes it's hard to tell. But often women are authors of profound emotions in poetry and narrative. They give voice to pains, joys, passions, loneliness, and struggles to understand relationships—all in the name of making something authentic and meaningful, often in spite of demons.

Among the contributors in this chapter, Joan Cusack Handler ushers in the ghost of her mother and transforms her deep feelings and yearnings into a universal language. Salita S. Bryant recalls Sex Ed at the playground. Claire Basescu writes a finely tuned lament about the shattering existence that begins at birth and accelerates as we age. Maggie Bloomfield declares her independence in a raw and fearless slam poem about empowerment. Another contributor writes amorously while her therapist is away on August break. Other contributors with an intuitive feminine perspective include Kim Bernstein, Amanda Hirsch-Geffner, and Gwenn A. Nusbaum.

Throughout history, women like Elizabeth Bishop, Maya Angelou, Emily Dickinson, and Sylvia Plath have breathed life and energy into their writing. Women should not be put on a pedestal or in a cage. In *Daddy*, one of the strongest poems ever written by a woman, Sylvia Plath, the feminist literary icon, uses apocalyptic metaphors to write about women kept in perpetual childhood by fathers and husbands. Plath expresses with increasing intensity the ambivalence of love and hate. "I was ten when they buried you./At twenty I tried to die." It has been said that the poem itself is having a nervous breakdown.

* * *

EVEN A PSYCHOLOGIST STRUGGLES TO COMPUTE
JOAN CUSACK HANDLER, PhD

Fifteen years she's gone, there's still
such regret—never enough
phone calls, secrets, girl talk;
she craved more; I kept her
safe an arm's length away—that chasm
I constructed to mute the bite of her
silence, innuendo, accusation.
Deep in the belly of that divide—the truth
of my divorce, clinical depression, loss of faith, and her
mother's death, loss of her brother, disappearance of her son—
    the one
I most regret—refusing to listen to her heartache.
Instead, safe talk of clothes, recipes, neighborhood gossip—a
    few giggles,
this time it's easy—she delightful—I'm moving closer,
even loving her … when
suddenly, the provocative child leaps, *You're the psychologist,*
why do you think I can never get enough from you kids?
"Well, Mom, you lost your mother when you were six." ***I never***
    told you about my mother!
she spits; the phone goes dead,
three weeks of silence,
Hi Joanie.

Joan Cusack Handler, PhD, is a poet/memoirist and a psychologist in clinical practice. She has published two poetry collections (*Glorious* and *The Red Canoe: Love in Its Making*) and a prose memoir (*Confessions of Joan the Tall*). Her latest book *Orphans* is a verse memoir. In her other lives, she is the founder and publisher of CavanKerry Press, lives in Fort Lee, New Jersey and East Hampton, New York.

FIFTH GRADE SEX ED
SALITA S. BRYANT, PhD

They almost certainly would never have said a thing,
except on the playground a brown-haired, bowl-cut boy
named *Tony something* had remarked that *the tomatoes
were growing* in a slurred hungry voice that spit with glee.
There was laughter at his gesture; hands splayed out
in front of his bony chest, flashed up and down, rocking,
mocking, as if he were trying

                              to juggle cantaloupe beneath
his shirt. He swayed, both knees bent, sauntering forward
into the crowd. All that year we had worked together,
making paper from pulp, extracting indigo dye from crushed
twigs, and forcing sugar to rearticulate itself into crystal
formations in mason jars. But who told or who saw
was a mystery. The playground held its collective breath
as he was culled from us,

                              pulled from behind the vestry
of that same church-school where I had been warned
not to ask the preachers any more questions if I was not
     willing
to bend my knee to their god. And so they separated us.
Separated male from female child, stalk from graft,
slit from slat—they split us at our roots—planted us in separate
rooms, so they could explain the other kind. And I sat there
looking at that anatomical poster

                              of a tame and tractable penis
that was as big as my arm, its head the size of my fist, that
     pearly
slit so mute. I sat there looking at these other girls, these
will-o'-the-wisps, these shoots of firewheel, with their delicate
petal faces lifted toward the bright high voice of that teacher,
thinking, how very surprised they would be to feel
the actual stir and prowl of such a nocturnal creature.

Salita S. Bryant, PhD, MEd, MFA, is associate professor of English, City University of New York and author of *Addie Bundren is Dead*. Winner of the 2013 Gradiva Award for poetry, she publishes widely, most recently in the *International Body Psychotherapy Journal*, *Boulevard*, *Agenda*, *Dogwood*, and *The North American Review*. She is a psychoanalytic candidate with Harlem Family Institute.

THE SHATTERING
CLAIRE BASESCU, PhD

1.
There is a limit to words
because one needs a body.
How long can I keep myself
warm with my mind?
The chill of autumn
frightens me.

2.
Old ladies haunt the streets.
Lined up outside
the lingerie store
with their walkers
and their sad determined faces.
Grief and loss
you do not want to think about.

3.
The lady poets save me
with their spirited quests
their not going gently
tenacious grip
that word-worship.
L. and S.*
and their "adventures"
Always riding over the top
of the bottomless sorrow.

4.
My Abby and her "personal death study"
as she called it.
Bright brave friend
tenderest of tough cookies
whose hospital roommate said
"she pitied the tumor that had to
contend with me"

and her
"life is good, despite everything."

5.
How do we
surrender
AND
fight?
Mustering energy out
of the long night.
Elusive dreams
that shatter as we try
to grab them.
Sometimes dazzling
Sometimes gone.

Claire Basescu, PhD, is a clinical psychologist and psychoanalyst in private practice in New York City. She is a faculty member and supervising analyst at the William Alanson White Institute and on the editorial board of *Contemporary Psychoanalysis*. She is the author of articles that combine scholarly, clinical, and creative writing on such topics as divorce, parenthood, abortion, and therapy.

---

*Louise Gluck and Sharon Olds.

SLAM POEM: TO THE VOICES IN MY HEAD
MAGGIE BLOOMFIELD, LCSW

I do not apologize to you.
I do not apologize to you.
I do not apologize to you.
Nothing I could say
could wash away
your indignation at my being me.
All you see
is not what you see,
what you want me to be.
If my eyes were brown
instead of blue,
It would not satisfy. You
want me down
and I am up, up, up,
designed to overflow
this cup of life,
regardless of how many no's
you hand me with supposed
affection focused on control.
I have another role.
Not daughter, friend, or wife,
not slave to negative ambition.
I have another mission—
to move, to dance, to grow
as tall as Redwoods if I choose,
despite your bullying
childhood taunts,
the labels that haunt
the porous nature
of my past and future.
The wild child you call slut,
resenting the guts I have
to navigate existence
without resistance.
It's your insistence
I drum from my mind,

unwind
the tapes of no, no, no,
refuse
to ooze into the mold
of old, old, old. I'm finishing
your diminishing
dismissing your idealizing,
your list of perfect features
that sabotages God's perfect creatures.
The message is the message:
It's a mess about age.
You clutter up my stage.
I'm whiting out the page
and covering it with rant.
Don't tell me I can't
transcend the ravages of growing old
with the power of my rage.
Your messages of no,
of stop and end must go.
I will not internalize
for I will be recognized
I do not apologize.
I do not apologize.
I do not apologize
to you.

Maggie Bloomfield, LCSW, MFA, a psychotherapist/writer/performer, is an Emmy winning lyricist for *Sesame Street*, and writes for musical theatre. Poems/essays are published in *The Southampton Review* (TSR), *PoetryMagazine.com*, *Grabbing the Apple*, *Psychoanalytical Perspectives*, *Montauk Anthology*, and the *Suffolk County Poetry Review*. Maggie runs writing workshops and performs spoken word locally and nationally.

TORPEDO
KIM BERNSTEIN, PhD

I am sitting with the sailboats
watching them turn on their watery dimes

counting quarters for coffee
counting the blessings of my life in this city

counting sailboats
noting the number of times

they turn toward the spot where I'm sitting
which is when it gets personal

much as I hoped it wouldn't
much as I wish to stay out of it

wanting to be invisible
wanting no one to notice

I'm twisting through loss
one in a series that blotted out summer
a whole season in shadow
though really just the tip of the iceberg

it will soon be cold enough to imagine properly
but that here in the late September sun

seems negligible, a glass-eyed metaphor.
And you are where you are

no longer required to navigate anything
recording your secrets, a soundtrack of whispering leaves

dancing along with the babes in carriage
who flail their limbs in delight of inscrutability

honoring the apes clearly manning this vessel
refusing comment on what's in the stars

what's now for you to know and us to find out
damn these torpedoes and full speed ahead.

Kim Bernstein, PhD, is a psychoanalyst in private practice in New York City. She is on the faculty at the Stephen Mitchell Center for Relational Studies and senior editor of *Psychoanalytic Perspectives*. Along the way, she earned her master's in creative writing from Temple University, and her poetry has appeared in such publications as *Talisman*, *To*, *Mass Ave.*, *Pom2 Magazine*, *YAWP*, *Peter O'Toole*, and the Academy of American Poets anthology *New Voices 2002*.

GABBEH

ANONYMOUS

People in therapy must inevitably deal with periods of time when their thera-
pist is away. Even though therapy is on hold, internal work goes on, and
writing can help keep the analysand balanced. At these times, we are artists
without our analyst. Those who find writing compelling turn to the written
word to hold the howling, swirling ideas racing through their heads—garbled
fragments that are too hot to approach.

I am Gabbeh. I take my name from an Iranian film, a story of a
nomadic young woman, haunted by longing for a man who appears as
a wolf howling on the horizon of her arid world. The "gabbeh" is the
rug she weaves while roaming the desert, aching to move toward the
sound of his cry. She weaves and she hopes, the design an elaboration
of her desire; the threads are of simple fibers, but the intricate patterns
begin to emerge, telling her story. I saw this dreamlike film in the second year of my analysis, during the arid time. In August.

This vast, parched terrain marked a transition for my inner landscape. I was, then, unaware of the life of tiny, undiscovered plants in
a desert-scape that hold the essential moisture for living. Two years
earlier: I dutifully carried in my first dream, of trudging through a
barren tundra. Could life be sustained in as bitter and unforgiving a
world as this? Was anything living beneath the drifting snow? If there
was nothing, I would starve. Yet I knew no hunger.

In the later Augusts of my long analysis, I spent the month
sailing the waters of New England, drifting off to sleep at night
on a gently rocking boat in snug anchorages with names like
Cuttyhunk, Fogland, and Smuttynose. How did I get here, from the
desert? I still listened for his howling—was he the wind that moved
me forward, sometimes gracefully, other times ferociously? I often
felt him in the watery surround that I moved within, where he was
velvety and soothing, but then wild and chaotic. But now my trust
in him grew so profound that the fear, the excitement and desire that
stirred in my heart became a sweet taste that called "More!" Yes, he
was the water that, after a long day I'd dive right into, by August
turned warm and welcoming to my tired and equally salty body.
Buoyant, free of the weight of the land-bound, I knew his presence
held me afloat.

In the perfect stillness of August sunrises, the water a mirror; or during a thrilling romp in a stiff southwesterly breeze, I scanned the horizon for him, knowing he was watching me, looking for him. Still, years past our goodbye, my eyes search, I know he is there.

It is August. I am Gabbeh, a flying carpet, carried by the wind, held by the sea.

ANONYMOUS is a psychoanalyst in private practice in New York City. A private person, she hopes her reflections on her experience in analysis will resonate for others who feel forever changed by the power of this transformative relationship; or to potentially inspire some whose passions are feared too wild.

MOURNER'S LITANY
AMANDA HIRSCH GEFFNER, LCSW

Dedicated to the memory of David I. Hirsch (February, 1926–October, 2004)

the look on my father's face while he waited for a train
or watched my one year old climb stairs,
his fat, cracked tongue
and the squeals of disgust and delight emitted by nieces
when it revealed itself over turkey and yams;
the way I sandwich memory of him
between thick leaves of wailing jazz on scratched LPs,
between the dear, the flawed, the unavoidable,

my father's farm-red house and his pink-slippered wife,
the marriage he left behind in the blue-shuttered house
of my learning to speak;
the way things went not according to plan,
engendering a mottling of random sarcasm
and kindliness to check-out clerks,
his imitation of a moose,
his "spouting whale in a suburban pool"

the apple and the ice-pack stored in vinyl pouch
vouchsafed to me
before they put him under one last time,
attachment to the hearty tugboats watched

while, in the other room, he puffed and slipped away,
and lingering,
my fear of open spaces left
when trains pass by

Amanda Hirsch Geffner, MA, LCSW, MFA, is a therapist at the Center for HOPE/ Family Centers in Darien, Connecticut, where she also facilitates bereavement and caregiver support groups. She enjoys zumba dancing, Torah chanting, listening to her son's DJ mixes, and watching her gymnastically gifted daughter do flips.

WOMAN IN THE WARD
GWENN A. NUSBAUM, LCSW

Don't blame her
if she must tuck herself
into small places—
a pocketbook
library corner
rocking chair,
boarding herself up
like an abandoned hotel.
She's really well-traveled—
been to Pluto and back—
and though modest
will tell you about it.

Gwenn A. Nusbaum, LCSW, BCD, is a relational psychoanalyst and trauma specialist in private practice in Manhattan. She received a Gravida Award nomination, Pushcart nomination and honorary mention for her poetry, which has appeared in several print and online journals including *Salamander, Diverse Voices Quarterly, Schuylkill Valley Journal, Rattle, and Louisville Review*. Gwenn also authored *Normal War*, a poetry chapbook.

CHAPTER SIXTEEN

Capturing moments: four very, very short narratives, three poems, and a photograph

C an we really capture a moment in writing—be it unspoken, spoken, or filled with an evocative image? Can we engage the creative unconscious in that moment and tap into our imagination? If we succeed, we are usually surprised at what turns up. Ernest Hemingway once wrote a story in just six words. "For sale: baby shoes never worn." And he called it his best work.

At the heart of things is chaos and it lives in our unconscious, where we learn to raid the inarticulate. We listen for the rumblings from those uncoded voices, and we translate them into our creative work, not in a literal sense but in a poetic metaphoric way. The writer has to be open to hearing those rumblings when they arrive, usually when she is busy doing something else.

While the unconscious mind plays, the conscious mind finds words and images to express the messages from the deep. As when the Greeks settled new colonies and always brought an urn filled with Greek soil to plant in the new territory, nothing is ever lost or forgotten. But the nature of the unconscious changes; it is continuously altered by experience. When we put pen to paper, the conscious mind makes choices and edits and turns these cryptic messages into writing. And something changes. It is an exhilarating moment.

When I give assignments to the writing groups that I have run for many years, I revise the old adage "Write what you know" into "Write what you *don't* know."

Language has a way of confining us. Writing is like wading at low tide. We walk along the beach and see worlds barely visible. "A world in a grain of sand, eternity in an hour." It's necessary to go to the edges of what we know about ourselves, then poke around that place, and be open to what we cannot see with normal vision. Interesting things happen around borders.

Write about bliss. About an upsetting moment when you realized you left something behind. About your father. The dinner table growing up. A moment that's very old and ancestral. In the groups, we write in the presence of others. From the ethos and the mist come beauty and ugliness, and surprising angels and devils. We dip our toes into the common pool of our humanness and the rich territory of our imagination—and thus enter the city of the new.

In this chapter, the authors capture large and small moments. We see imagistically a chance encounter with mannequins in Barcelona, and read about one woman's fleeting relationship with a bird. Other pieces are about childhood imagination, nostalgia, and unconscious doodling. They all transport us.

It is through artistic expression over eons that we are able to appreciate our common humanity—what makes us laugh, what makes us cry, what fills us with wonderment. Like the plays of Sophocles and Euripides, Chaucer's *Canterbury Tales*, the Renaissance paintings of Raphael and Da Vinci, a piano concerto by Mozart, the cave paintings in France and Spain from 35,000 years ago. Through their creative works, they allow us to touch them, to feel their presence, to hold their dreams. They allow us a glimpse of who we were. It is through their art that we inherit our civilization. And it is through *our* art that future generations will know us.

* * *

FINITUDE

ROBERT D. STOLOROW, PhD, PhD

If we're not self-lying,
we're always already dying.
If we're not self-deceiving,
we're always already grieving.
The answer to the existential quiz?
"Good-bye is all there is."

Robert D. Stolorow, PhD, PhD, is a founding faculty member and training and supervising analyst at the Institute of Contemporary Psychoanalysis, Los Angeles, and a clinical professor of psychiatry at the UCLA School of Medicine. He is the author of more than fifteen books and 200 articles. He received his PhD in clinical psychology from Harvard in 1970, and a PhD in philosophy from the University of California in 2007. He received the Hans W. Loewald Memorial Award in 2012.

DOVE? GULL? GULLIVER?
VALERIE OLTARSH-McCARTHY, LCSW

It was one of those extremely windblown, frigid nights that we get here on Riverside and 73rd. I'm walking into the wind with my two Fairway bags, feeling pretty sure that a few of my fingers are going to be casualties to my love for fingerless gloves.

I get to the door, slither down the steps into the lobby, and Jeff says, "Valerie, is that your bird?" I turn around, and a dove or a gull or something has flown in with me and has landed at the bottom of the stairs.

I get down on the floor with the bird and start telling her she's a really sweet bird but the stair landing isn't the best place for her. She looks around, unconvinced, especially given the contrast in weather between West 73rd Street and the lobby.

Then I realize how convenient it is that I got crackers at the store. I break one up and put it far to the side of the lobby. She doesn't really perk up at my culinary offering, so I slide the cracker toward her. Not interested. Several of my fellow cooperative shareholders enter, glance at me on the floor with the dove, and continue on their way, impassive.

It's really feeling like time to get upstairs and have my dinner. I scoop up the bird, we go back out into the bitter cold, and I place her on the ground next to me. "I'll stay here with you to make sure you get off okay," I say. Well, actually, after about a minute or so, I renege on that and go back inside. Sorry, you're on your own. But the bird flies in with me, again, and lands on the lobby floor.

Marie then comes in, and I say, I have this problem with this bird who keeps flying in with me and now I'm going to have to bring her upstairs. Would she have a shoe box to help with the transport? Marie goes upstairs and comes down with something like that, so I scoop the bird in and bring her upstairs with me.

So now it's like 9:15 at night, and I have this wild bird in my apartment, and I haven't had dinner, and I'm really not so sure what to do. She's really cute and she's kind of flapping around, and I name her Gulliver. That's when you're really screwed, when you name the animal who found you on the street.

I have this epiphany as Gulliver starts to take wing to my living room walls and I start worrying about bird concussion and prospective human sleeplessness. I can make Marie's shoe box into something of a lean-to, place it on my terrace, and put a bowl of water and some soaked crackers inside. So then Gulliver can have shelter and snacks, and fly off when she's ready.

I prepare the bird accommodations and set her inside, and make sure the box is secure and the flap will stay open. Then I get a towel for the bottom so she can be cozy. I retreat to the inside of the windowed terrace door and watch. She nibbles. Fifteen minutes later, she's still there. And fifteen minutes after that. And after that. Then she's gone. I miss her, white body, orange beak and feet. I kind of would have liked her to stay; maybe we could have worked something out.

Fifteen minutes later, Gulliver's still gone, and still after that, and so then I can go to sleep. At three o'clock, I get up and turn on the terrace light, and she's still gone and I'm sad and smitten.

Get up early the next day. Go out to the terrace. Gulliver's back. She'd come home to die in the early morning.

Valerie Oltarsh-McCarthy, LCSW, is in private practice in Manhattan. She is a graduate and faculty member of the National Institute for the Psychotherapies. Beyond a real fondness for humans, she delights in her relationships with animals, and in traveling throughout the world.

ARCHITECTURAL IRONY—BARCELONA, 2008
JANET GOLDMARK, LCSW

While basking in the architectural splendor of Barcelona, home of Gaudi and Miró, I was captured by the irony of this vision:

Janet Goldmark, LCSW, MFA, has a background in the fine arts which she credits for the creativity of her spirit. Janet has been a practicing psychoanalyst in New York City for the past thirty years. She is a supervisor and the former clinical director of the Child and Adolescent Training Program at the National Institute for the Psychotherapies.

VISITING SAVTA BOBBE IN TEL AVIV
OFRA BLOCH, LCSW

In the beginning I thought God lived behind the door at 35 Rashi Street in Tel Aviv, where Savta Bobbe lived.

Savta is *grandmother* in Hebrew, and Bobbe is *grandmother* in Yiddish. Savta Bobbe was my great-grandmother, so my name for her was not altogether inaccurate. For as long as I can remember, I was taller than she was. Her size turned out to be quite convenient, as she shared the tiniest two-room apartment with her daughter, my great-aunt Mera, and Mera's husband, Binyamin.

The two-hour drive from Jerusalem to Tel Aviv took plenty of preparation and seemed like a great voyage that would last forever. We would make the journey in summer, and when we arrived, exhausted and thirsty, Savta Bobbe would immediately serve us a hot cup of tea, for she firmly believed that this is the only way "to chase away the heat." In Savta Bobbe's household nobody cared about table manners. Binyamin used to drink his soup while producing distinguished sound effects, but for some unknown reason he was allowed such imperfection, even by my father.

Binyamin owned a barbershop, and I was thrilled when I could spend the day there, looking at pictures of beautiful hairdos in foreign magazines, eavesdropping on the conversation, smelling all those weird hair lotions, and listening to Binyamin whistle whole concertos. He always wanted to treat me and would get frustrated by my refusal. "How can anyone refuse food?" he would wonder, nodding his head and wrinkling his brow in bewilderment. "And especially sweets …"

When I accompanied Binyamin on errands, he would tell me stories about his time in the concentration camp, but instead of a solemn and harrowing narrative, his tales were always about the pranks he had played on the camp authorities. To me, it sounded like such a fun place, and I couldn't help but wonder why my parents did not have stories of their own about similar camp hijinks. When I learned that my parents in fact had not been in the camps, I thought that perhaps they hadn't been good enough to be sent there.

Savta Bobbe thought that neither my mother nor I could ever do any wrong. I doubt whether she would have approved of our secular way of life, but she chose not to know what she didn't want to know.

On Saturday evening she would send me to the balcony to look for three stars in the dark sky, the signal that the Shabbat was officially over. There was a lot of tension around this issue because my secular parents just wanted me to turn on the lights, an act prohibited until the end of Shabbat. The whole family would wait impatiently in the dark, nagging me to hurry up, till Binyamin would roar in his deep voice, "Oh, say, can you see the comet?" But I took my job seriously and would reply with the self-confidence of a six year old, "A comet doesn't count as a star."

At night I used to share a bed with Savta Bobbe, and she would lullaby me in Yiddish. She'd sing *Oifen Prepetchik* ("By the Fireplace"), and I would dream about the sounds and smells of a place I'd never been to. Maybe it was her shtetl.

When Savta Bobbe was not plucking chickens for Friday night's soup, which was her main domestic activity, she busied herself with praying. By the time I was a teenager, she rarely left the house. She would stand in the corner of her room behind the opened door, tiny woman that she was, dressed in her traditional long polka-dot dress, her hair tightly covered, her blue eyes closed, and pray to God. Later on I was told that Savta Bobbe never ceased to pray. She prayed in the midst of the pogrom in her hometown in the Ukraine, she prayed on the boat that carried her and her five newly fatherless daughters to Palestine, she prayed when the Turks who ruled Palestine at the time expelled them to Egypt, she even continued to pray when her eldest daughter died of typhoid, leaving behind her a two-year-old who grew up to be my mother.

I was away from the country when Savta Bobbe passed away. Upon my return, I rushed to her home and peered behind the door. The space was tiny and would have fitted comfortably only her and God. Both were absent.

Ofra Bloch, LCSW, is in private practice in New York City and is a supervising analyst at the National Institute for the Psychotherapies. She is also a documentary filmmaker and her feature, *Afterward*, which explores the theme and experiences of meeting "the other," is currently in production.

BLUE

EDWARD McCRORIE, PhD

A single bluefish moves from the sea toward land
over a spread of off-green stones and sepia
tangles of weed. They rise like a headland.

A starfish below cannot prey on the blue,
for the star's fixed and the blue is see-through
fin and resolve, outlined beauty and scale.

About half done with it, Ellen stares at them. Though
vexed and intrigued, she'll likely discard them,
what with a dozen pick-me-up cries from the other
cranky sketches lying about her.

She's loved Old Lyme's shoreline in summer, alone,
wrongly anxious, likely, about her husband
cruising fast from New York to Bermuda.

Edward McCrorie, PhD, is professor emeritus of English at Providence College in Rhode Island. He has published six books of poetry as well as translations of Homer's *Odyssey* and Virgil's *Aeneid* with Hopkins and Michigan Presses. His present works include a translation of the *Prophecy of Jeremiah* from the ancient Hebrew. He is married to Beatrice Beebe, a psychoanalyst and infant researcher in New York City.

THE LITTLEST THERAPIST
EMILY LEVIN, LCSW

When I was a little girl, around six or seven, we had a neighbor who was a therapist and saw patients in her home. I was fascinated. I would race home from school, park my stool in front of the kitchen window, and stare at the patients walking in and out of her house. I wanted to know everything about what happened inside. I would observe the patients with wonder. What was wrong? What were they talking about? How did they get to my neighbor's house? Where did they work? Did they have a little girl? Did they like ice cream? I had a million questions. I would make up stories about the patients, but somehow the stories did not seem to help me figure out what happened inside my neighbor's home. I was dying to figure this out. So, I decided I would become a therapist, and then I would know what happened.

My room became my office. I set up my desk with my pink plastic phone on top and my bills and notepads inside. I dressed in my mother's heels. Overalls and heels made for an interesting therapist uniform. I would put my dolls on my bed, and they'd talk about their feelings. They would ask questions, and I would give them answers. I spent hours in my office. One day my father arrived home from work and knocked on my office door. "What's going on in there?" he wanted to know. "Your mother says you have been up here for hours." I walked to the door in my heels and overalls and announced, "Dad, I am a therapist. If you want to talk, schedule an appointment."

My phone began to ring off the hook. My father, my grandfather, my aunt—they all wanted to come in for some shrinking. My father set up an appointment with me and arrived the next day. He came right after work and did not even stop to take off his suit and tie—he was eager to get started. I instructed him to lie on my bed. There he was in his suit and tie lying on my bed with my dolls and blankie. He was my patient on my analytic couch. I was soooo excited. My dad started, "Well, Dr. Levin, I have come to see you because I have this issue that has been on my mind, and I was hoping you could provide me with some answers."

"Okay," I replied. He continued: "So I have this issue, Dr. Levin, and I don't know what to do. I have this little girl who sometimes does not like to clean her room, and I am not sure how to get her to clean it." "Daaaaaaaaaaaaaaaaaad!" I screeched. "You are not supposed to talk about me; I am the therapist." I guess at the time I did not know how lucky I was that my first analytic patient was willing to talk about the transferential relationship and the real relationship at the same time and in the first session. "Dad, you know I can give you an answer that I really think will work." "Yes, Dr. Levin," my father exclaimed with great enthusiasm. "Please tell me!" "Just tell her to clean her room." "Okay, Dr. Levin. That is brilliant. I am going to try it, and I will get back to you next week."

I gave my father a bill, and we scheduled another appointment. My father paused at the door for a moment before leaving. I was a little nervous that he was going to ask me to clean my room. "Dr. Levin," he said. "Yes, Dad?" "You are a very good therapist, and you have a beautiful office." The door closed, and I sighed with relief. I guess therapists don't have to clean their rooms, I thought. This job could work for me. I braced myself for dinner that night—I knew my dad would ask me to clean my room. I thought to myself, I hope that we don't talk about his daughter at his session next week.

Emily Levin, LCSW, is a psychoanalyst, psychotherapist and certified EMDR therapist. Emily is a graduate of the National Institute for the Psychotherapies Four-Year Program in Psychoanalysis, as well as the Trauma Certificate Program. Emily is codirector of the NIP Psychotherapy Evening Program. She has a private practice in Manhattan and Brooklyn serving children, adolescents, adults, and couples.

EVENING COMMENCEMENT
ROGER SALERNO, PhD

An old man sings what could be his last song
As he makes his lonely trek through the cool evening desert.

It is an aria from an opera he once imagined he had written in
    Italian
When he was a twelve-year-old boy.
But he never learned Italian, so he never actually wrote it.

As he stands alone and sings his song (in his best voice)
Into the dark desert sky,
He suddenly finds himself enveloped
By a brilliant constellation of stars.
And he knows each one of them by name.

And his song suddenly turns into a chorus
With music streaming from the dark heavens.
But there are no real words to the song
Rather only a deeply felt sense of connectedness—
That *oceanic* feeling Freud could never find.

And he realized that something magical had just happened
That could never happen again.
And he would be changed by it forever.

Roger Salerno, PhD, is a psychoanalytically trained sociologist who teaches at Pace University in New York, where he specializes in social theory and gender. He has written five books and numerous articles. His latest book is about young boys who lived on the streets of Chicago in the 1920s.

REGENERATIONS
JENNIFER CANTOR, PhD

Their reunion occurred on an unseasonably warm winter's day under the arch at Grand Army Plaza. They embraced awkwardly, jabbering nervously about the fine weather and impressive architecture, finally settling into an easy stroll and a familiar silence. Released from the shroud of cold, dark days, they let nostalgia lead them on a long walk down Ocean Parkway to the Coney Island Aquarium. There they stood side by side, gaping at the undulations of the jellyfish, its dance across their reflection as light as chiffon.

They had met more than a year before in a greenhouse in the mountains. For days they stooped over hundreds of spinach seeds, their nimble fingers pressing each tiny seed into the enveloping earth. Then they lovingly wrapped a fig tree in layer upon layer of discarded newspaper, branch by crooked branch. They read the headlines aloud to each other as they worked, and laughed that their tree was swaddled in scandal. He loved to watch her laugh, though he glanced at her only when she wasn't looking, so that she never knew he studied and memorized her face. She reminded him of his wife, whom he hadn't seen in thirty-five years, of his daughter, whom he'd seen only once. Life, he told her, had knocked him to his knees, and he'd spent the last twenty years closer to the earth than most people get.

She too had tread perilously close to life's parameters. Her exile had taken her from India, where young goats sacrificed their heads to a bloodthirsty Kali, to Siberia, where the vengeful earth had cut her bare feet as mercilessly as razors. Stumbling haphazardly into his greenhouse, she'd discovered there throbbing relief.

One year later they were walking arm in arm along the boardwalk at Coney Island, mismatched, perhaps, but upright, and grateful. Her thawed feet barely touching the ground, she leaned over and planted a gentle kiss on his weathered and whiskered cheek, sealing it with her palm. In silent, satisfied unison, they turned to watch the waves tirelessly unfurling on the shore.

Jennifer Cantor, PhD, is a clinical psychologist and graduate of the NYU Postdoctoral Program in Psychotherapy and Psychoanalysis. She is in independent practice in Vermont.

CHAPTER SEVENTEEN

Ferenczi and relationality: on losing one's analyst

Sandor Ferenczi, a Hungarian psychoanalyst and intimate of Freud until he was ostracized from Freud's inner circle, placed an inordinate emphasis on the concept of mutuality. For him, the cure was in the relationship, and he introduced for the first time a two-person psychology in which patient and analyst become mutual partners in a reciprocal relationship within the analytic hour.

My interest in Ferenczi is also a personal one. My training analyst, Emmanuel Ghent, was analyzed by Clara Thompson, who herself was analyzed by Ferenczi. When we trace our analytic ancestry back through time, we can discover our unconscious family tree. We are great-grandchildren in the lineage of psychoanalysis as one generation's unconscious is passed down to the next.

Recently, there has been a growing appreciation of the importance of Ferenczi's contribution, and his influence on the evolution of modern psychoanalysis. In his *Clinical Diary* he allows us to experience moments between him and his patients where the "analytic encounter is curative." Ferenczi emphasized that the interaction between analyst and analysand was primary, and in his practice he engaged in a high degree of self-disclosure.

With the importance of relationality in mind, in this chapter we look at two narratives evoking the loss of an analyst after many years of treatment. In the first piece, "Ode to Jerry," Darcy Dean Minsky writes about the horror of losing her analyst right in front of her eyes. The second narrative, "Breaching the Walls," is Kabi Hartman's account of a patient's struggle to hold onto the memory of her analyst after learning that he had died.

My analyst also died when I was in treatment. I was devastated to lose him, and I never had a chance to say goodbye. He was gone in the real world, but eventually I became able to summon him when I need him. For him, time is up, but in my being, our time is endless. If one can invent a clock, one can invent time. And at the end, like Michelangelo, he became just a man like any other.

* * *

ODE TO JERRY: WHEN THE FRAME CRUMBLES
DARCY DEAN MINSKY, LCSW

Jerry was my analyst for twenty-one years. Under his guidance, I left the acting profession and graduated from social-work school. I married, had two children, and began a private psychotherapy practice. I lost both of my parents, survived cancer, and began a training program at a psychoanalytic institute. Through all of these life changes, Jerry was there.

I had come to know Jerry as an orderly person. His clothes were well worn and casual and his shirts were starched. He kept his office clean and well organized, with current issues of magazines neatly arranged on a table. Jerry was conscientious about time and religious about beginning and ending sessions punctually. He had a talent for seamlessly ushering one person out of his office and the next person into his office in fewer than thirty seconds. In that way, each person was still within his or her forty-five-minute hour.

He had arranged his office hours according to New York City's alternate side of the street parking regulations. He would stake out a parking spot on the street near his office and then read *The New York Times* while waiting in his car for his parking spot to become legal. He knew the deli guy on the corner and the homeless man who trolled the street. He immersed himself in psychoanalytic theory and began to write a book. He gained weight, grew his hair, which was turning silver, and began to wear a beard.

Jerry was unconventional. In warm weather he could be seen riding his rusty bike around the neighborhood with a rubber band fastened around the bottom of his pant leg. One day I remember waking up in the hospital recovery room after having had an emergency appendectomy. At that moment I realized that I was supposed to be at Jerry's office for my weekly appointment. So I asked the nurse for a phone and called him to explain my situation. My hospital happened to be down the street from Jerry's office, so he came to visit.

Part of Jerry's unconventional style was sharing information about himself. He had adult children living across the country. He had a grandchild who was close in age to my daughter. He lived in a house upstate. His cousin was a dentist. At the time I accepted the disclosures as a part of who Jerry was.

Some would consider Jerry's disclosures a breach of the psychoanalytic ground rules also referred to as the "frame." The frame defines the physical and psychological space where analyst and patient interact. These rules are created to ensure safety and to foster trust. When ground rules and boundaries are established, the two parties explore, create, and exchange personal meanings. This happens in the overlap of two play areas, that of the patient and that of the therapist.

The psychoanalytic frame that Jerry and I had constructed provided the ground rules, the overlap of play areas, and the sense of safety. The angles of the frame were not always set at ninety degrees, yet in spite of its asymmetrical design, the frame felt sturdy and dependable.

And so it went. Schedules and routines were in place, and our meetings continued throughout the years until the twenty-first year. That's when I began to experience a feeling that things were somehow different. Suddenly I realized that there was no one in the waiting room before or after my session. Uncharacteristically, Jerry began showing up late to my appointment, claiming that there had been a lot of traffic on the highway.

One day, while sitting in his waiting room, I noticed something out of the corner of my eye. It was a Chinese restaurant menu perched atop the wastebasket. It felt familiar. Had I seen it there last week? I looked around, and noticed that the furniture hadn't been dusted and the bathroom floor was sticky. Later, as I sat across from Jerry in his office I could see that both pant legs were wet. It had not been raining.

I didn't say anything to him, but consulted a friend who is a doctor. My friend said that Jerry's behavior and his wet pants indicated a serious condition that required immediate attention. During my next session I told Jerry what I had observed and what my doctor friend had said. I asked him about his wet pant legs. He smiled and responded by saying that he was having a problem with his prostate. I asked him if he had been to the doctor. He laughed and said no. I tried to convince him to seek medical attention. I reasoned, demanded, and pleaded, but he only smiled and dismissed my concerns.

My world was shifting. The sharp, clear lines that had once defined Jerry were dissolving into a pointillist's indistinct dots. His image blurred behind my tears. I had depended on him and trusted him to hold my thoughts and my feelings. I had counted on seeing his face and hearing his voice every week. He understood the details of my life.

They were his thoughtful words that I heard when I was confused and frightened. Again I expressed my concerns regarding his behavior and his physical state, and tried to offer him help. Again he smiled and dismissed me. I did not know what to do. My hope was that he would snap out of it. But as the days passed, he became more disheveled in his appearance and his pants were regularly wet. He did not seem uncomfortable, nor did he appear self-conscious. I can only assume that he was unaware. The Chinese menu remained perched on the wastebasket. During my sessions he related childhood memories and reminisced about his younger years as an officer in the air force.

The frame had crumbled. The portrait of the analyst and the patient no longer existed. The frame had provided us with roles and a purpose. He was the analyst. I was the patient. We had a designated time and place to meet every week. I spoke. He listened, reflected, interpreted. But now the frame was broken, and I did not want to see what lay in the rubble.

It was clear to me that Jerry was fading away. I was frightened and wanted to do something. I had to do something. I knew that he was living alone at the time, so I decided to call his cousin, the dentist. I had to look up the cousin's name and number in the telephone directory. What was I doing? I knew that I was breaking a cardinal rule, but I couldn't stop myself. I didn't care. When I finally contacted Jerry's cousin, he expressed irritation at my intrusion. He informed me that he no longer spoke to Jerry and that no one else in the family wanted to have anything to do with him, including his own children. The cousin-dentist didn't care about Jerry's diminished state.

I contacted social services in Jerry's town. His phone had been disconnected due to failure of payment. A worker went to his home to assess his status. Jerry refused her help. She told me that there was nothing to do. She had seen worse. She said that the rights of the individual are strongly protected in our society, and that a person has the right to live in chaos.

Though Jerry was no longer able to function as my analyst, I had decided to continue meeting with him. I would watch over him until I could figure out what to do. Ashamedly I wrote out a check to him every week and sat across from him, smiling and nodding as I listened to his stories. One day at the end of my session, he asked me to join him for a "cocktail." It was time to end the charade. I tried to gently explain to him that I could no longer meet with him. He looked at me through confusion and surprise. He shrugged his shoulders and smiled. "Okay. If that's what you want," he said.

But that was not what I wanted! I wanted everything to be the way it had been. I wanted Jerry to answer the buzzer in his funny way. I wanted to see him sitting in his brown leather chair next to his dimly lit lamp. I wanted him to always be there, waiting; the constant in my life among all of life's changes. He was the person that I could always go to, but what was I to do now? All I could do was say goodbye. I remember him standing in profile as I left his office. His silver hair was long and full. He wore a playful grin, and there was a twinkle in his eye.

Though I didn't meet with Jerry, I continued my vigilance. I kept in touch with his caseworker and occasionally called him on the phone to see how he was doing. He was chatty and playful during our conversations. He said that his health was fine and then he asked if I were calling to schedule an appointment. He must have been confused by my phone call. In the past my phone calls to him were to schedule an appointment, ask for guidance, or to seek assurance. But on this day I had called to inquire about his well-being.

Over the next few months I learned that Jerry had lost his house through foreclosure. The new owners had hired a moving company to carry his beloved books, manuscript, furniture, clothes, shoes, and other worldly possessions onto the sidewalk. From there, a storage company packed up Jerry's possessions and carted them off to storage units. The caseworker was there to oversee the dismantling of his home and assured me that the procedure was legal.

I couldn't bear to imagine Jerry standing on the sidewalk in front of his home. Yet I continued to ask the caseworker questions in an attempt to fill in the details of the scene. Perhaps I could restore the image of the Jerry that I had once known. Maybe there was some detail that I had overlooked. But the picture of Jerry remained distorted. I had to stop.

One night, about six months later, as I was driving home from work, my husband called me on my cell phone. The caseworker had called to say that Jerry had passed away. He had been living in his office and was discovered by the building's superintendent.

It is four years later, and I am left with the task of trying to figure out what went right and what went wrong. I struggle with the respect that I have for the psychoanalytic ground rules and the love I had for my analyst, who was ailing and alone. I only wish that I could have helped to save Jerry's life the way that he had saved mine.

Darcy Dean Minsky, LCSW, MS, is a graduate of the Dual Degree Program between Bank Street College, Special Education Program and Columbia University School of Social Work. She is also a graduate of the National Institute for the Psychotherapies (NIP), Child and Adolescent Psychoanalytic Training Program. She currently works at a public school in Hoboken, New Jersey.

NAMING THE ABSENCE
KABI HARTMAN, PhD

Seven o'clock on a Wednesday night in May 1990. I am lying on the plush purple couch in Dr. E.'s office. The track lights have been dimmed, and although the blinds are drawn on all three windows of the corner office, the headlights of cars going west on 91st Street cast undulating shadows on the white wall above me. These Wednesday sessions, cocooned inside this familiar room, I feel most alone with Dr. E. In the twilight I have less trouble saying everything that comes to mind: I speak fluidly and confess things I never thought I would say to anyone.

We are discussing my extreme attachment to Dr. E. Death is on my mind—his, in particular. *But what would I do if you died?* I am working myself into tears, preparing to leave the consulting room the way I often do—in a ferment of passion, slamming the door, exiting the building, and scraping my knuckles against the bricks of the apartment buildings on Central Park West. Outside, on the street, two male voices joke as they pass by the windows. It is spring, and Dr. E. and I are both young: He is in his thirties, I in my twenties. Yet the possibility of his death looms, as the fear of my mother dying haunted my childhood.

From the darkness behind me, Dr. E. finally speaks: It would be a bummer, he admits.

His choice of word, with its vague association to drugs—a bad trip—defuses my looming histrionics. As I write this, older now than he was that night, I conjecture that Dr. E., who usually did not speak until ready to offer the perfect interpretation, was tired. Mine was the last session of his day, and he probably wanted to go home to his wife. At that moment, his own death seemed remote to him, a mere bummer. But today, eight years after Dr. E.'s untimely death, I am glad for the echo of those words. They are so inadequate and offhand; they make him seem unafraid. I think he might enjoy them too, if he were around to remember.

If someone had warned me that night that Dr. E. would die suddenly of a heart attack in May 2001 at the age of forty-eight, seven years after I concluded my analysis, I would have been certain that I would not survive his loss. What I could not imagine then was that my consuming need for Dr. E. would retreat down the dark hole from which it had burst at the beginning of my analysis. At the time of his death, I was already in Pennsylvania, a doctoral student and adjunct professor, a wife and a mother. I had found a normal life—one that seemed inconceivable to me during my analysis years.

I rarely mentioned my analysis. I was keenly aware that while I lay on the couch free-associating, my peers had been finishing graduate school, raising children, rising in their fields—things I had not had the energy to do then, and was therefore only just beginning to accomplish. And I also felt tentative about revealing how indelibly my analysis had marked me. Pressing at the edge of my present existence, my seven-year analysis needed to be acknowledged. Yet when I mentioned it to friends, they were puzzled. *Five days a week? For seven years?* My experience of analysis was locked away in Dr. E.'s consulting room, preserved but out of bounds.

And then one early summer evening in 2001, I returned home from a party to a message on my answering machine from Dr. E.'s colleague. Dr. E. was dead. He had collapsed in a parking garage on a Saturday morning the week before. He was a few paces from the emergency room at Lenox Hill Hospital when he died, on his way to seek treatment for his increasingly severe breathlessness.

In the days that followed, I realized my unique isolation. Because it had been difficult to notify all of his former patients in time, I heard about his death more than a week after it happened and therefore missed his memorial service. This loss of the chance to mourn him communally was the first intimation of what I was going to have to grapple with: In some profound way that I could not yet articulate, I was left on my own. There was no social context for my loss, as no one in my life had ever met Dr. E., and only the few of my friends who had been in intensive therapy themselves understood my abiding attachment to him. Although I was aware that there were many people mourning Dr. E.—his family, friends, colleagues, and patients—none of them knew of my existence. My grief was permeated with the awareness, familiar to me from my analysis, of my anomalous relationship with Dr. E. In the wake of his death, I began to plumb that relationship again, trying to answer the question of how and where he fit into my life.

My life as a patient began when I was twenty-four years old. Living with one man but in love with (and having sex with) another, my days had become overwhelming. When the three months of free sessions available to me as a graduate student at Columbia University were almost up and I had reached no satisfactory resolution to my problem, my therapist there suggested I start psychoanalysis with a psychologist whom she knew to be highly qualified and who—more to the point—had hours available for a student who could pay very little.

I wore a faded red T-shirt, worn black jeans, and red ballerina-style shoes to my first session. For half an hour before I finally rang his buzzer, I sat on a bench on Central Park West smoking Camel Lights and listening to Elvis Costello's *Imperial Bedroom* on my Walkman. The white-noise machine in Dr. E.'s waiting room hushed the echoes of Costello's plangent anthems but did nothing to mute the din of my anxious thoughts or slow my accelerating heart rate. I was convinced that I had embarked on a journey that would change me forever.

My nerves spiked as I heard Dr. E.'s consulting room door open and his footsteps on the hall rug. And then there he was, smiling at the edge of the waiting room: a short Jewish guy in his mid-thirties with a kind face. Dr. E.'s warm and eager smile, along with his youthfulness and the white shirt and chinos he wore, struck me as inappropriate. He looked too nice, too sporting, not intellectual enough. I had imagined an aloof, cigar-smoking graybeard. How could someone like this analyze me? Yet when Dr. E. offered me his hand, my composure vanished. I did not want him to know how nervous I was, but contact with my cold, clammy hand would reveal all.

In Dr. E.'s consulting room, I summarized my romantic difficulties blithely, conscious of turning on the charm for my new male analyst. I left the office vaguely disgusted with myself, my hands now hot and clenched, hating Dr. E. for having made me false.

But I returned the following week. It was a rainy early summer morning, cool but not cold. Sitting once again in Dr. E.'s office, I tried to talk to rather than perform for him. It was a beginning; and a few weeks later, Dr. E. handed me a schedule of my analytic hours for the following year. He and I had agreed—inevitably, it seemed to me—that I would come to his office five times a week, beginning in September, to be analyzed.

But of what did I need to be cured? Was I in any worse shape than many people in their early twenties? What gave me the idea that understanding myself was the key to my happiness?

These questions still baffle me. My decision to devote seven years of my early adulthood to such a strict form of therapy sometimes seems to have been overkill. But to say this is easier than to admit that I needed help. My three months of therapy at Columbia Health Services had brought to mind events that I had tried to forget. There was my grandfather, who had allowed me and my sister to pull back his covers and view his penis every morning of our summer vacations. There was my boss—my father's best friend—who had grabbed and French-kissed me late outside the café where I waited tables. There was my father, who liked to describe the specific ways his former girlfriends had experienced orgasm. There was the college professor who had put his jacket around my shoulders, invited me to brunch, and sent me a valentine. I needed to understand how these happenings, and others like them, continued to affect my relationships with men.

I wanted to understand other problems in my life, too. Why had I been so angry and self-destructive in sixth grade—scaling the railing on the boardwalk outside my fancy private school and dangling myself over the East River, or brandishing a pair of nail scissors and covertly cutting fellow students' and teachers' hair when we were all crushed together in the elevator? And why, when I was sixteen and starved myself down to seventy-eight pounds, did my parents fail to notice? Why had my mother seemed so happy one windy day in January when she took too many muscle relaxants and thought she was finally, blamelessly, dying? Why had my father had a series of affairs? Why, at twenty-four years old, was I so emotionally distant, such a liar, so unable to accept my own wants?

Almost as soon as my analysis began in September 1987, I developed a transference, the predominant feature of which can best be described as a reprise of the powerful attachment I had to my mother when I was two years old. I wanted Dr. E. all the time, and was content only in his presence. I felt bereft on Friday nights, when the week was over and I knew I would not see him until Monday morning. To distract myself these evenings, I often visited a friend in Brooklyn Heights. There was one brownstone on Court Street that compelled my attention; the blinds on its front windows were always open, allowing me to gaze into the living room. I pretended that Dr. E. lived amidst the track lights and leather chairs, the exposed brick walls and quietly bubbling aquarium. Standing outside on the street, I was spellbound by the intensity of my wistfulness, the yearning itself standing in for Dr. E. in his absence.

On the surface, though, my life settled down during those seven years. I finished my master's degree and kept working the secretarial job that had paid the bills while I was at Columbia. My romantic life burgeoned as I left the man I had been living with and moved into an apartment with the man I had fallen in love with. We had two cats, several great friends, a loft bed, and a television set. We raced home from our Peruvian chicken at Flor de Mayo to watch the latest episode of *Twin Peaks*. Eventually we got married.

However, the turbulent real story of these years took place within the walls of Dr. E.'s consulting room. Psychoanalysts say that a good analysis is partly forgotten, and for me this is true. When I think about my own, I find I cannot recall much that was actually said unless I reread my journals from that time. Rather, I remember the routine: the expectant walk down Broadway, the countless weekly magazines read in the waiting room, my right leg crossed over my left as I lay on the couch, the scone I always bought on my way back uptown. The emotional tone of those seven years has stayed with me more than the specific insights: just walking into the supermarket where I then shopped, just smelling the metallic odor of the arctic freezer in which I used to select pints of Häagen-Dazs ice cream, brings back the intensity with which I daily lived, the swollen eyelids and aching chest. Of course I recall the therapy dramas—my lacerating jealousy when Dr. E. took two weeks off after becoming a father; the strange shame I experienced when I met him on the street or in a favorite brunch spot—but while the distress of these occurrences has diminished with time, the recollection of his gentle voice has not.

And then one day I was thirty, still working as a secretary. I had put everything on hold so that I could focus on my analysis, but suddenly felt sidelined. Sometimes as the sky turned to dusk outside my office, I caught a glimpse of my reflection in the large window. Then I would stare at my face and wonder how it was that I, who wanted so much to be a writer and teacher, had become a secretary? My husband had finished graduate school and was starting a job as an assistant professor in Lancaster, Pennsylvania. It was time to leave.

Six years later, pregnant, I took the train back to Dr. E.'s familiar office on Central Park West twice a month to talk about becoming a mother. I was researching my dissertation then, and often stood at the copy machine in Columbia's Butler Library after these sessions, marveling at my huge belly. After I gave birth, Dr. E. and I saw each other or talked on the phone at least once a month. His keen interest in my experience of motherhood touched me.

Our last session took place the Friday a week before Dr. E. died. I was telling him about the physical problems I had suffered after childbirth (postpartum gallstones) when he confided that there had been a time in his life when he too had felt fragile on account of serious health problems: a herniated disc and then hepatitis. I leaned forward and pointed a finger at him immaturely: *You're not allowed to die*, I said out of the blue.

I left his office that day feeling unsettled and unaccountably sad. Although I was unaware of it then, I later found out that Dr. E. had recently visited his doctor to discuss a persistent feeling of breathlessness. He was worried about his health, and his anxiety had communicated itself to me.

I fantasized about Dr. E.'s death frequently the summer after he died. I imagined him driving himself into Manhattan from his house in Riverdale to the parking garage where he had collapsed. I wanted to inhabit his body until I too grew short of breath; I wanted to feel his clammy hands grip the steering wheel; I wanted to knock my frame against the concrete floor of the garage. Some part of me had to die with him. But my fantasy did not stop there. I conjured his body covered by a white sheet on a stretcher, his familiar Rolex watch and gold wedding ring perhaps already plastic-bagged to be taken home by his wife with his other belongings. I imagined that Dr. E. had been an organ donor, and pictured him being delicately sliced open in a lab. I envied the people who had received his eyes or kidneys. I wanted to be included in any part of his death I could have.

Mourning Dr. E. took up most of my free time that summer. I stopped working on my dissertation and wrote in my journal, using the babysitter time to sit in my brown armchair in my pajamas. I turned to books for comfort, rereading the few I could find in which a patient writes about his or her analysis. Eventually I began to write about mine.

However much I may balk at the idea, I know that I cannot shape the story of my analysis and Dr. E.'s death without leaning heavily on the interpretive frame he himself provided for me. For seven years of my life Dr. E. helped me to construct my own story; in his terms, he was my "co-author." Now, eight years after his death, I am haunted by the fact that only my side of our mutual story remains. Dr. E.'s clinical notes on my analysis have been destroyed, but I live on, teaching, mothering, writing, speaking, and remembering. Perhaps as I bear witness, Dr. E.'s voice still speaks in mine, helping me to breach those closed walls and retrieve those fruitful years.

Kabi Hartman, PhD, is senior adjunct assistant professor of English and director of the Spring Admit Program at Franklin & Marshall College in Lancaster, Pennsylvania. Her work can be found in such publications as *Western Humanities Review*, themillions.com (where she has written about the depiction of therapists in young adult literature), and 2para-graphs.com; she has an essay about her analysis in *The Point* magazine.

INDEX

209

For Product Safety Concerns and Information please contact our EU
representative GPSR@taylorandfrancis.com
Taylor & Francis Verlag GmbH, Kaufingerstraße 24, 80331 München, Germany

9 781782 204602